Praise for *Free in Deed*

"A wonderfully lucid treatment of what Christian ethics is, here fine-tuned to all the core themes of Luther and Lutheran traditions. The consequence is a splendid exposition of neighbor love lived in freedom for a planet in peril."

—Larry Rasmussen, Reinhold Niebuhr Professor Emeritus of Social Ethics, Union Theological Seminary, New York City

"Craig Nessan has created a vital resource for the church. It is a thorough, deeply faithful, insightful, and vibrant exposition of Lutheran ethics as an emancipatory mode of being people of God. Particularly important are his clear differentiation between conventional meanings of freedom and a Lutheran Christian understanding of freedom and his concise argument that Luther's teachings about two kingdoms—often misinterpreted to justify separation of religion from political engagement—call Christians to political engagement in service of the neighbor. This book will be invaluable in both classroom and congregation!"

—Cynthia Moe-Lobeda, professor of Christian ethics, Pacific Lutheran Theological Seminary and Graduate Theological Union; director, Center for Climate Justice and Faith (PLTS); author of *Resisting Structural Evil: Love as Ecological-Economic Vocation*

"Craig Nessan provides us with a concise and compelling introduction to ethical reflection in the Lutheran tradition. Instead of a tired litany of Lutheran catchphrases, this book creates a conversation for the purpose of speaking a word to the challenges that face our world today. Nessan's voice allows readers to find their own as they respond to neighbors and people freed and forgiven in Christ."

—Anthony Bateza, associate professor of religion, St. Olaf College

"*Free in Deed* is timely, Lutheran to its core, and accessible to all who want to connect their faith to their daily lives. It will be a welcome addition to the core curriculum of synodical lay schools, as well as the academy."

—Greg Kaufmann, assistant to the bishop, Northwest Synod of Wisconsin, ELCA

FREE IN DEED

FREE in DEED

THE HEART OF LUTHERAN ETHICS

Craig L. Nessan

Fortress Press

Minneapolis

Contents

Introduction

On the Study of Ethics

THIS BOOK SERVES AS A PRIMER in Lutheran ethics for the faith and life of the church as the body of Christ. It is fruit from teaching ethics at a Lutheran seminary for more than twenty years. More than that, however, it flows from research and reflection on Christian ethical existence over the course of my entire career. The title of the book, *Free in Deed: The Heart of Lutheran Ethics*, is based on the Gospel reading for Reformation, John 8:31–36, where we read, "So if the Son makes you free, you will be free indeed" (8:36). What Martin Luther made clear about Christian freedom is that it has two crucial dimensions: (1) freedom *from* everything that holds us in bondage from being the persons God created us to be and (2) freedom *for* serving the neighbors God gives us to love in all our roles and relationships. When Jesus Christ sets us "free *indeed*," we are set free to serve others "*in deed*." The heart of Lutheran ethics involves serving neighbors. While this focus is not unique to Lutheran ethics, I contend in this book that it is the most distinctive feature of ethics in Lutheran perspective.

From the outset, I want to clarify and underscore that the references to "neighbor" throughout this book should be interpreted expansively. As "neighbors," we must include other Christians or people of faith, of course. But all people in their diversity—each and every one—need to be encompassed within the horizon of our ethical concern. In order for this ethic to embrace *all*, for Christ's sake, we always are called to privilege those who are most at risk and in danger of being disregarded as neighbors. This is the preferential option for marginalized people. In our times, we see many categories of persons who are in danger of being treated as "disposable people" by systems of power. Even more, I insist that whenever we employ the term *neighbor* in this volume, we reference not only all our human neighbors but the neighborhood of all creation. Creatures, plant life, and the entire natural world must always inherently and inextricably belong to our understanding of *neighbor*. The human experiment on this planet and the welfare of future generations depend on our upholding the integrity of creation.

My own formation as an ethicist has been decisively shaped by the christocentric thought of Dietrich Bonhoeffer, whose witness as a disciple of Jesus Christ has provided ongoing orientation for the journey. Early on, the voices of liberation theologians grabbed my attention as a compelling embodiment of what Christopraxis means at this moment in history, confronting us who live at the center of empire with a world where many persons exist on the periphery, whose lives are considered disposable. To these witnesses have been added in my own formation many prophetic voices, not least of all from the radical theology of John D. Caputo and Catherine Keller. This journey has led me to expanding of horizons to incorporate the well-being of all creation—minerals, flora, and fauna—within the scope of God's purpose to enact *shalom*. All our neighbors! *Mitakuye Oyasin!* All our relatives!

The call to the ethical life originates with the primal question posed by God as much to us as to our ancient ancestors: "Where are you?" (Gen 3:9). Each moment and every day throughout human history God searches our thoughts, words, and actions, calling us to locate ourselves in relationship to our Creator and the neighbors God gives us. As with our original parents, we too prefer hiding ourselves from God's presence. However, with the psalmist, we are reminded how God examines the heart:

> Where can I go from your spirit?
>> Or where can I flee from your presence?
> If I ascend to heaven, you are there;
>> if I make my bed in Sheol, you are there.
> If I take the wings of the morning
>> and settle at the farthest limits of the sea,
> even there your hand shall lead me,
>> and your right hand shall hold me fast.

> If I say, "Surely the darkness shall cover me,
>   and the light around me become night,"
> even the darkness is not dark to you;
>   the night is as bright as the day,
>   for darkness is as light to you. (Ps 139:7–12)

The ethical life encompasses all of one's human existence from beginning to end and in relationship to all creation. Ethical existence always transpires *coram Deo*, "in the presence of the Living God." Though we may try to deceive ourselves, there is finally no place to hide.

Defining Ethics

The origins of the words *morality* and *ethics* derive from the Latin *mores* and Greek *ethos*, respectively. The terms refer to the shared beliefs and practices of a given people. Each society has certain standards and expectations for behavior, conventions about what is good and evil, right and wrong. These can be known through the precepts of the law or through proverbs instilling wisdom. The *mores* and *ethos* are instilled through a socialization process that unfolds in the family, through experience, in education, and by life in society. Today we might refer to these as the measures of "conventional morality," ways of living assumed as "normative" for people in a given culture. Lawrence Kohlberg once identified "conventional morality" in American society as conforming either to "interpersonal concordance" (where being good is what is pleasing to the majority of people) or to "law and order" (where being good means doing your duty in society by obeying laws and respecting authority).[1]

We offer here a formal working definition of ethics as discussed in this book. *Ethics as a discipline involves intentional and disciplined reflection, together with a community, on the choices we must make in living our lives in the world.* There are four notable features of this working definition. First, in contrast to conventional morality, ethics requires that we slow down our pace to allow conscientious thought and deliberation on the course of our lives: thoughts, words, and actions. Second, ethics is not merely an individual activity. Rather, ethics requires that we test our reasoning with others, who can assist us in clarifying and correcting our path. These others may include not only the persons to whom we are connected by social bonds but also the voices of those who have gone before us and are represented by a tradition. Third, ethics is not optional. Every day we make thousands of decisions, many of which we never pause to consider. The momentum of routine and the pace of life often overtake our consciences, distracting us from taking the time necessary for thoughtful ethical responsibility. Fourth, the ethical life is embedded within a world of local, regional, national, and global circumstances that condition and limit what may be possible. The weight of these forces may threaten us and cause us to despair about the difference we can make in the larger world. We must claim our ethical agency within the complex web of cause and effect to which our efforts contribute incrementally to the common good.

While this working definition also can apply to philosophical ethics as pursuit of the good employing nonreligious categories, the scope of this book focuses on theological ethics in relation to life lived in the presence of the Living God (*coram Deo*). Christian ethics, therefore, becomes life in the presence of the Living Jesus Christ (*coram Christo*). Bonhoeffer writes that Christian ethics "is God's reality revealed in Christ become real . . . among God's creatures, just as the subject matter of doctrinal theology is the truth of God's reality revealed in Christ."[2]

In Christian ethics, we pay special attention to Jesus Christ as the bringer of the kingdom, crucified, raised from the dead, ascended, and present by the power of the Holy Spirit. This is what Saint Paul meant by "life in Christ" (Rom 8:2), life under the influence of the Spirit of Jesus Christ. This entails not only that our lives await some future judgment by God, as on the last day when Christ "will come to judge the living and the dead," but that our every moment is transparent to God's presence in Christ. Accordingly, Lutheran ethics becomes one particular tradition within Christian ethics, generated from the writings of Martin Luther and the Lutheran Confessions, interpreted within their historical contexts, including Scripture, and retrieved for the life of Christians and the church today.[3]

One of the remarkable features of the biblical narrative is how these books are written under the assumption that God is a living Actor before whom "we live and move and have our being" (Acts 17:28). While we today may not have the same palpable sense of God's immediacy to our daily lives, that does not contradict the reality that God in Christ is active in our world and that our lives are ever open to God's inspection. In contrast to how biblical characters conducted their lives *coram Deo*, we are much more inclined to measure ourselves *coram mundo* (in the presence of the world). Our occupation veers toward how our lives look before others, for example, on camera or according to a virtual persona on social media. We measure our lives quite differently depending on the audience to whom our attention is pitched.

While there are no pure types, ethical systems have been classically sorted into three types. The first and most prevalent understanding of ethics is based on rules, a *deontological ethic*. Here the ethical life is organized in relationship to laws that place limits on bad behavior and provide a guide in aspiring to good behavior. In the Christian tradition, the Ten Commandments are the foundational formulation of a deontological ethic. The natural law tradition, most fulsomely developed in Roman Catholic moral theology, was also operative in the thought of Luther.[4]

The second type orients the Christian life toward desirable goals, a *teleological ethic*. Depending on what has been determined as the most desirable outcome, one entertains the complexity of circumstances in order best to approximate that purpose. This orientation was famously epitomized by Augustine: "Love God and do what you will."[5] Situation ethics is one example of an ethical approach that sets love as the highest good and seeks to align the ethical life toward fulfilling that end.[6]

The third type focuses on the development of character, an *areteological ethic*. This derives from the Greek word *arete*, meaning "excellence" or "moral virtue." Here the ethical life is oriented toward instilling habits of being that shape human beings as actors in the world to express themselves nobly. This ethical approach is grounded in the philosophy of Aristotle and the theology of Thomas Aquinas. It has been given new articulation in our times, especially in the work of Alasdair MacIntyre, and has become significant also for Lutheran ethics.[7] This book draws from all three types in constructing ethics in Lutheran perspective.

The traditional location of ethics in the theological curriculum has been in relation to dogmatics. In general terms, works in dogmatics (teaching about Christian doctrine) articulate the meaning of the Christian faith, while ethics interprets the significance of these teachings for the Christian life. This pattern was already established in the nineteenth century—for example, in the works of Friedrich Daniel Ernst Schleiermacher and Lutheran theologians such as Johann Christian Konrad von Hofmann and Friedrich Bauer.[8] Prominent twentieth-century Lutheran contributions in this pattern were written by Paul

Althaus, Werner Elert, and Helmut Thielicke.[9] The fragments by Bonhoeffer published posthumously as *Ethics* deserve special attention as original contributions forged in the crucible of the church struggle in Germany.[10] More recently in North America, there have been texts used for the teaching of Lutheran ethics, but none as extensive as the works already noted. George Wolfgang Forell, Karen L. Bloomquist and John R. Stumme, William H. Lazareth, Oswald Bayer, and Walter Altmann have each contributed volumes useful for the teaching of Lutheran ethics, but each also has particular limitations.[11] Forell, Lazareth, and Altmann give primary attention to Luther's own theology, whereas Bayer and Bloomquist/Stumme provide essays in Lutheran ethics rather than a more extensive approach.

Orientation to This Book

This book provides a comprehensive text on fundamental topics in ethics from a Lutheran perspective. I contend that Lutheran ethics is finally neighbor ethics. The gospel of Jesus Christ sets us free to serve neighbors—including all creation—and their well-being. This introduction serves as a brief orientation to the field of ethics with special attention to a Lutheran portrait. Each of the eight chapters builds on the previous to give readers an understanding of both the distinctiveness of a Lutheran approach and the implications for the discipline of Christian ethics ecumenically.

Chapter 1 on "Biblical Authority and Lutheran Hermeneutics" names Scripture as the chief authority in Lutheran ethics and explores six core themes: (1) God speaks, (2) the finite bears the infinite, (3) the privileging of the "literal sense," (4) law and gospel, (5) Christ as the center of Scripture, and (6) the proper use of hermeneutical reason, including a method of interpretation for Lutheran ethics. The entire chapter contrasts with two false directions: literalism and subjectivism.

Chapter 2 on "The Authority of Tradition, Reason, and Experience" elaborates three other sources of authority for Lutheran ethics. Tradition involves negotiating the meanings of Scripture in subsequent generations under the assumption that texts contain a "surplus of meaning."[12] This means that the church always is challenged to discern legitimate from illegitimate readings in an ongoing "conflict of interpretations."[13] Creeds, confessions, and doctrines function as forms of tradition. Reasoning on the meaning of texts involves the incorporation of insights from other disciplines (sciences, social sciences, and the liberal arts) into ethical reflection. Scientific consensus positions are of particular value for drawing ethical conclusions. Experience is the most humanly accessible but also ambiguous source of authority and needs to be tested by the other sources.

Chapter 3 on "Gospel Freedom in American Context" first explores conventional meanings of freedom in the American context as they refer to lifestyle choices, political rights, the economic system, and military defense. None of these are congruent with the specific meaning of Christian freedom, which can lead to gross misunderstandings when we talk about "freedom" in the context of the church. This is further illustrated through the work of David Foster Wallace. Finally, the chapter elucidates Christian freedom in Lutheran ethics with reference to Luther's *The Freedom of a Christian*. The Lutheran understanding is twofold: (1) freedom from everything that holds us in bondage and (2) freedom for service of neighbors. Neighbor love is the entire purpose of Lutheran ethics.

Chapter 4 on "Luther's Two Kingdoms as God's Two Strategies" acknowledges the tragic misinterpretations of Luther's two kingdoms teaching. In intentional contrast to a localized and static kingdom metaphor, the two kingdoms perspective is reinterpreted constructively as God's two strategies, both of which aim to bring forth the kingdom (*shalom*) of God. The right-hand strategy involves second use of the law, the means of grace, the gospel as the source of Christian freedom, the work of the Holy Spirit, and the sending into service of neighbors. The left-hand strategy involves ministry in daily life through service to one's family, in daily work, in the local community, through public church, and by citizenship.

Chapter 5 on "Justification and Sanctification" stresses the centrality of justification by grace through faith in Christ alone within Lutheran ethics as generating freedom for service of neighbors. Lutheran ethics has struggled to articulate the nature of the Christian life, what other traditions often interpret as sanctification. Several categories are used to describe the Christian life in Lutheran ethics, including (1) the third use of the law, (2) renovation in Lutheran Orthodoxy, and (3) living faith in Lutheran Pietism. The proposals by Bonhoeffer for "costly grace" and by the Finnish school (Tuomo Mannermaa) on the indwelling Christ provide the most promising constructive approaches. Unlike a Reformed focus on personal holiness, Lutheran ethics insists on neighbor love as the consequence of the Christian life.

Chapter 6 on "Vocation of the Universal Priesthood" affirms the universal priesthood as the unfulfilled promise of the Reformation. The gospel of Jesus Christ sets us *free from* every form of bondage that prevents us from being the persons God created us to be and *free for* serving neighbors in the arenas of daily life. Our responsibilities to family, daily work, local community, public church, and citizenship are the primary arenas for living out Lutheran ethics. The "churchification" of Christianity functions as a contemporary Babylonian captivity contributing to the church's decline. Renewal of the church involves the formation, equipping, sending, and scattering of the baptized to live out Christian vocation in daily life. Baptism is the primary ordination. Worship practices are life practices that form Christians for this vocation.

Chapter 7 on "The Ethics of the Cross" asserts that Lutheran ethics is carried out under the sign of the cross. We need to beware tendencies toward both trivialization and triumphalism of the cross. Suffering can be differentiated among three types: (1) suffering inherent to the human condition, (2) suffering caused by some and imposed on others (structural injustice), and (3) suffering that the Christian church chooses to take upon itself for the sake of the neighbor. This third type of suffering is specific to an ethics of the cross. With reference to Luther's theses at the Heidelberg Disputation, the chapter reflects on the recent proliferation of texts on theology of the cross, including the work of liberation theologians.

Chapter 8 on "Luther's Two Strategies and Political Advocacy" demonstrates the usefulness of the two kingdoms framework for engaging in political advocacy. According to Lutheran ethics, Christians are called to work together and build coalitions with all those who share commitments to the common good, whether those allies are Christian, of other religious faiths, or neither. There are not only two uses of the law in Lutheran ethics but also two uses of righteousness, reason, will, and works. This offers an original interpretation of Lutheran political advocacy as "neighbor politics" in contrast to the "religious identity politics" of much of American evangelicalism. Luther's two strategies paradigm offers a distinctive contribution to the work of political advocacy.

In the book's conclusion on "The Ethics of Forgiveness," we acknowledge how all ethical engagement transpires under the conditions of sin—whether personal or structural—and cries out to God, neighbors, and all creation for forgiveness. We exercise the ethical challenge of forgiveness between two poles: the experience of unforgivable sins and the universal command of Jesus to forgive. Forgiveness is facilitated under the conditions where the offender demonstrates remorse, repents, and makes amends. Forgiveness is complicated by the lack of these conditions. Forgiveness in this world remains, therefore, a process awaiting eschatological resolution.

Gratitude

This book has been forged through my engagement in the teaching and learning community at Wartburg Theological Seminary. I am grateful to faculty colleagues, students, and alumni who have engaged this material critically and constructively through the course Ethics in Lutheran Perspective, now called Lutheran Ethics. I acknowledge with appreciation the permission to include as chapters in this book significantly revised versions of material previously published (see the copyright page for a detailed listing).

This book is dedicated to all those working toward the prevention of child abuse and advocating vigilance by faith communities for policies and practices that safeguard child protection. Above all, this includes Victor Vieth, director of Education and Research of the Zero Abuse Project, and his colleagues there, including Suzanne Severson and Robert J. Peters. I also name in this dedication the contributions of Shira Berkovits and Basyle Tchividjian, authors of *The Child Safeguarding Policy for Churches and Ministries*; Marcia Bunge from Gustavus Adolphus College; Cindy Miller Perrin and Robin Perrin from Pepperdine University; Carrie Walker Nettles and Shauna Galloway-Williams of the Julie Valentine Center; Pete Singer of Care in Action Minnesota; and all those devoted to advocacy for the protection of children from harm. I am profoundly grateful for how they are contributing to the transformation of theological education, including at Wartburg Theological Seminary.

1 Biblical Authority and Lutheran Hermeneutics

HOW SHALL WE THINK ABOUT AND reclaim biblical authority for the life and mission of the church in our time? This is a foundational issue facing the field of ethics, given that Scripture is its primary authority. This is an especially urgent challenge for ethics in Lutheran perspective, with its focus on *sola Scriptura* (Scripture alone). This chapter explores six theological affirmations for interpreting the Bible according to a Lutheran hermeneutic. These themes are grounded in the Lutheran Confessional tradition and informed by key insights from hermeneutical theory. This approach can help map a course for renewing the interpretation of the Bible for creative ethical engagement.

The Holy Bible is vast, mysterious, and rich with unexplored depths. Consisting of thirty-nine Old Testament writings and twenty-seven New Testament books, the Bible's various genres of literature are like ecological niches within the whole, each worthy of attention. At the same time, the Bible strangely continues to speak to each new generation with inexplicable power—God's Word transcending the particularities of space and time. We find ourselves at a time when many Christians have lost fascination with this holy writing and biblical illiteracy is on the increase. Our culture has largely lost even cursory familiarity with the biblical narratives.

False Directions

How does the contemporary context complicate our approach to biblical interpretation? I will employ the metaphors of undertow and tsunami to describe two inexorable forces that distress biblical interpretation. First, we need to recognize the mighty undertow (rip currents) of postmodern approaches to Scripture, such as reader-response criticism or deconstruction, both of which forefront human subjectivity in the process of interpretation. As a school of literary criticism, reader-response approaches focus on the reader and the reader's idiosyncratic "experience" of a written text.[1] This can be contrasted with those approaches that pay strict attention to the authorship, form, and content of a work. The primary actor in the interpretation of a text becomes the reader, who lends the text meaning through an act of creative imagination. Reading is a performing art, through which each reader creates his or her own unique text-related performance. The text means what it means to "me."

Deconstruction also shifts attention to human subjectivity in the process of interpretation.[2] Committed to the premise that language is incapable of communicating anything about what "is" (being), deconstruction analyzes the limits of language by making comparisons between things and pointing out differences. Deconstruction analyzes texts with the suspicion that authors—wittingly or not—disguise metaphysical assumptions to serve their own privileges through their writing. Deconstruction is a strategy of interpretation for disclosing inherent contradictions and unmasking false claims. Like reader-response criticism, deconstruction shifts the focus from a text's content to the subjectivity of the interpreter(s)—however, not in celebration of human creativity in the act of reading but with suspicion about unwarranted assumptions and self-interest hidden in texts.

Both reader-response criticism and deconstruction are approaches in which the meanings of texts are "underdetermined." That is, we approach texts not in order to discover *what is being talked about* but rather to pay attention to the subjectivity of the one who is doing the talking. These approaches reflect, although differently, the hyperindividualism of the postmodern. All claims for shared meaning as communicated through writing and every assumption of metanarrative are subject to the power of an undertow that draws us under the waves to drown every claim to universal significance, including theological claims about God and God's activity.

A second overwhelming force with which we contend is literalism.[3] Biblical literalism emerged in the nineteenth century and was strengthened by the development of fundamentalism in the early twentieth century. Since that time, biblical literalism has, like a tsunami, been washing away the nuance and intricacy of other modes of interpretation. Literalism has been fostered among many church members through its prominence in the media (TV evangelists) and "Christian" literature. While literalism does allow for metaphor and parable in some Scripture passages, it is committed to the literal occurrence of the described events. Biblical literalism is grounded on belief in the inerrancy of the Bible, guided by the conviction that the original "autographs" (manuscripts) were inspired by God in such a way as to make them free from error of every kind.

Many biblical literalists distinguish true from false Christians according to well-defined litmus test issues: abortion, homosexuality, creationism, and climate change denial. Literalism famously insists on the historicity of biblical stories—for example, a six-day creation or forty-day flood. Such belief leads literalists to oppose evolutionary science as conflicting with biblical creationism and to understand apocalyptic texts (e.g., in Daniel and Revelation) as predictive of events that will actually take place in the end times. The refusal to engage scientific findings, particularly related to the devastating consequences of climate change, contributes paradoxically to the actualizing of perilous end-time scenarios depicted in the literature of millennialism. Christian dispensationalism is embedded within an apocalyptic worldview, in which unconditional support for the State of Israel, amid conflicts in the Middle East, accords with the Bible's predictions for the end times.[4]

If the meaning of texts is underdetermined in postmodern approaches to the Bible, it is even more the case that the meaning of texts is "overdetermined" by biblical literalism. Clearly defined theological commitments about the nature of Scripture and divine truth predetermine the meaning of particular Bible passages. These commitments were codified in the "five fundamentals," which define fundamentalism: the inerrancy of Scripture, the virgin birth and deity of Jesus, the doctrine of substitutionary atonement, the bodily resurrection of Jesus, and the premillennial second coming of Christ. Fundamentalist theology concentrates on "propositional revelation," the doctrines and teachings that God has revealed to humanity in the Bible and that the faithful are expected to believe and defend. This is a highly rationalistic approach to Christian teaching. Based on its convictions about Scripture, fundamentalism rejects all forms of "higher criticism" that investigate the origins, sources, and historical development of the biblical books in favor of "plenary inspiration" to the biblical writers by the Holy Spirit. It is important to recognize how the theological commitments of fundamentalism predetermine what the Bible "must" say.

As Lutherans chart a course for interpreting God's Word in Scripture, we navigate between the undertow of subjectivity found in many postmodern approaches and the tsunami of objectivity demanded by biblical literalism. How can we steer between an underdetermination of meaning on the one side and the overdetermination of meaning on the other?

Six Theological Affirmations for Biblical Interpretation

God Speaks! (*Deus dixit!*)

Genesis 1:1–3 says, "In the beginning when God created the heavens and the earth, the earth was a formless void and darkness covered the face of the waters, while the spirit of God swept over the face of the waters. Then God said, 'Let there be . . .'" God speaks and it happens! This is the heart of the first creation story. The spirit enlivens God's Word and things come into being: light, sky, earth and vegetation, the heavens, creatures of sea and sky, animals of the land, and even human beings. Six days of creation. God speaks and creation happens!

The witness of Scripture to the efficaciousness of God's Word is plentiful. Perhaps the most frequently cited (and misunderstood?) text about the inspiration of Scripture is 2 Timothy 3:16–17: "All scripture is inspired by God and is useful for teaching, for reproof, for correction, and for training in righteousness, so that everyone who belongs to God may be proficient, equipped for every good work." Notice how the force of this text is directed at what inspired Scripture has the power to do—teach, reprove, correct, train—what Scripture *does* to those who hear.

Where does the inspiration of Scripture lie? Is inspiration rightly understood as the dictation of the words by God to the original amanuensis? Is inspiration manifested in the pages of a book? The doctrine of verbal inspiration (and its corollary, inerrancy) arises at the originating fissure where the tsunami of literalism is generated. On the other hand, is inspiration confined to what the reader makes (or does not make) of a biblical text? Is each classical text equally inspired as a biblical text? The undertow of certain postmodern readings would make the meaning of inspiration vacuous.

We here develop an alternative view called "dynamic inspiration." God remains ever sovereign in the event of inspiration; God does not deposit inspiration in the Bible as a manual codifying divine truth. Instead, inspiration remains an event that God created then, and God creates ever anew at the confluence of the proclamation of Scripture, our hearing, and the arrival of the Holy Spirit. Inspiration is a verb, not a noun. It is an event that God brings to pass in the reading, teaching, and preaching of God's Word by the power of the Spirit. The church must continually implore God to send the Spirit to our interpreting the Word, what Yves Congar describes as an ongoing "epiclesis."[5] We pray that God continues to speak to us through this Word as to people of old: "Come, Holy Spirit!"

This dynamic understanding of inspiration, inspiration as event, belongs to Martin Luther's own view of how God acts through the Word. Luther distinguished between the outer word and the inner word. The outer word is Scripture, while the inner word is "God's own voice by his Spirit. Without this inner word of God the outward word remains a letter, the word of man." Regin Prenter articulated well Luther's own dynamic view of the inspiration event: "When we hear the Word of the Scripture, we are compelled to wait on the Spirit of God. It is God who has the Scripture in his hand. If God does not infuse his Spirit the hearer of the Word is not different from the deaf man. No one can rightly understand the Word of God unless he receives it directly from the Holy Spirit."[6]

Luther, in contrast to his scholastic opponents, refused to understand the inspiration of the word *ex opere operato* (i.e., as automatically or, some would say, magically). Likewise, Luther's view differs from every concept of verbal inspiration. Luther's understanding of inspiration is "realistic" and dynamic, not "idealistic," by which "revelation is at the mercy of the one who *has* the means of grace."[7] Hearers of the Word must await and anticipate God's ever-new act of bringing Spirit to the Word in our presence.

If the Bible is replete with evidence internal to Scripture about the efficacy of God speaking through the Word, is there external evidence for the claim that "God speaks" through the Bible? The primary external evidence for this claim is the existence of believers themselves. In every generation, the church has testified to the power of God's Word giving her life. God continues to engender and foster faith in the lives of those "who hear the word of God and obey it" (Luke 11:28). The very existence of the church as a community gathered around the Word of God witnesses that God continues to speak through the Bible and its proclamation thereof.

The Finite Bears the Infinite (*Finiti capax infiniti*)

While it was in the controversy about the nature of Christ's presence in the Lord's Supper that Luther most ardently defended the thesis that the finite is capable of bearing the infinite, this affirmation is consistent with his view of the relationship between the human and the divine in Scripture. Against Zwingli, Luther insisted that God employs earthly means to bear Christ to the world. Christ is really present—not just spiritually or symbolically present—in the bread and wine.[8] Luther was emphatic about this claim because at root, the incarnation itself was at stake. How human was Jesus? When the Scripture says that "the Word became flesh" (John 1:14), how should we understand the relation of the divine God to human matter? Luther's Christology insisted on the very divine presence in the fleshly humanity of Jesus Christ. Just as Jesus himself was fully human—a baby at his mother's breast, weeping at the death of his friend, suffering death by crucifixion, and lying in the tomb—so Jesus Christ's body is fully and really present in the bread of Holy Communion.

George Wolfgang Forell makes the connection between Luther's defense of the finite as bearer of the infinite in the sacrament and his understanding of the Bible: "The implications of this emphasis upon the significance of the finite as a medium of God's revelation is clearly seen in the conviction that the bread and the wine of Holy Communion are simultaneously the body and blood of Christ, and, perhaps not as clearly to many Lutherans, that the human words of Paul and Peter are the Word of God."[9]

Ahead of his time, Luther intuited the complex historical process according to which the Bible acquired its form. Therefore, Luther employed what we have come to describe as elements of historical criticism to interpret the biblical text.

Willem Jan Kooiman describes Luther's approach:

He was convinced that various prophetic books (as well as some epistles) were not written by the men whose names were attached to them, but were rather assembled by redactors. The book of Ecclesiastes, in his opinion, does not come from the hand of Solomon. When one of his table companions remarks that in the judgment of many the Pentateuch was not written by Moses, Luther asks, "What does it matter?" Elsewhere he gives expression to his conviction that many of the laws credited to Moses existed long before his time. . . . Nor was Luther silent about difficulties arising from a comparison of the Gospels, since they do not always agree in details. The Passion history, especially, he regarded as "extremely confused" at various points.[10]

Clearly, Luther as professor of Scripture understood that the Bible developed in a process subject to the vagaries of human authorship and redaction. Luther's own method of biblical interpretation legitimates what we have come to describe as historical criticism, that method investigating the historical circumstances of authorship, the use of source material, the process of editing texts, and so on.

While Luther opened the door to scholarly investigation of Scripture, he also continued to insist that God speaks through this very human book. Even without a doctrine of verbal inspiration, Luther upheld a profound respect for the authority of the living voice of God speaking through the human words of the Bible: "He was concerned about a dynamic and functional understanding of the Word of God that happens now, rather than a legalistic manipulation of a once-and-for-all inspired book."[11] Just as Christ is both true God and fully human, the Bible is both Word of God and fully human words. Luther wrote,

> Holy Scripture possesses no external glory, attracts no attention, lacks all beauty and adornment. You can scarcely imagine that anyone would attach faith to such a divine Word, because it is without any glory or charm. Yet faith comes from this divine Word, through its inner power without any external loveliness. It is only the internal working of the Holy Spirit that causes us to place our trust in this Word of God, which is without form or comeliness.[12]

God chooses to come to us in a finite, fragile vessel.

Privileging the Literal Sense (*Sensus literalus*)

Because of the distortions of Scripture interpretation exacted under the authority of pope and councils, Luther insisted on the authority of Scripture alone (*sola Scriptura*). Whereas in classical medieval exegesis, there developed a fourfold approach to the interpretation of Scripture, Luther gave priority to the "literal" (or "plain") sense of the text. In the fourfold medieval approach, the literal sense at times had been considered inferior to the allegorical (pointing to the text's doctrinal importance), moral (pointing to the text's meaning for the individual's life), or anagogical sense (pointing to the text's eschatological meaning). Luther employed the literal sense of a text to regulate all other readings:

> One must deal cleanly with the Scriptures. From the very beginning the word has come to us in various ways. It is not enough simply to look and see whether this is God's word, whether God has said it; rather we must

look and see to whom it has been spoken, whether it fits us. That makes all the difference between night and day.[13]

Luther gave the literal sense of Scripture priority over all symbolic or mystical readings.[14] This privileged the obvious "literal" meaning of the text in its context.

Luther's commitment to the literal sense was based on his belief that the Scripture is "perspicuous."[15] This means he believed that the Bible's meaning would be clear to those who were (finally!) free to read it in their own language. We recall the significance of Luther's German translation of the Bible, making God's Word accessible to the public in an unprecedented way. Luther's confidence about the clarity of Scripture was grounded on his theological conviction that the entire Scripture points to Christ. The message of the Bible, both Old and New Testaments, finally is a message that foretells and proclaims the coming of Jesus Christ and the gospel. Moreover, Scripture mediates the gospel of Jesus Christ as its central message to readers and hearers yet today. This is most certainly clear!

In those passages where the meaning of the Bible is confusing or ambiguous, Luther employed the principle that "Scripture interprets itself."[16] Because the Bible is its own highest authority (in contrast to Rome and the enthusiasts who appealed to other authorities), one searches the whole counsel of Scripture to shed light on obscure texts. Insofar as the meaning of Scripture is clear in its witness to Christ and the gospel, Luther trusted the Holy Spirit to enlighten the interpretation of disputed texts that need to be understood through the lens of those that are crystal clear. This is a principle of interpretation that still deserves our attention as we wrestle with passages about which there is no agreement. How do we appeal to passages about which there is widespread consensus as we navigate the significance of contested texts for the life of the church?

With the emergence of modern historical critical methods, discernment of the literal sense of Scripture has become increasingly complicated. Sorting through the voluminous—and often conflicting—claims by scholars can be overwhelming. Moreover, we are confronted with Rudolf Bultmann's dictum that "exegesis without presuppositions is not possible."[17] Nonetheless, to provide a baseline for all subsequent interpretation, it remains useful and even necessary to begin with the literal sense of Scripture as the normative starting point. In this context, "literal" sense refers to the effort to understand *how a given text functioned in the life of the earliest community to which it was directed.* This definition allows for and authorizes the use of a range of exegetical methods, each of which can contribute to the retrieval of the literal sense of the text.

Law and Gospel (*Lex et evangelium*)

A distinctively Lutheran contribution to the ecumenical conversation about biblical interpretation involves use of the law-gospel paradigm to understand what God says to us in Scripture. This is a particularly Lutheran *theological* proposal within the history of interpretation. Luther recognized God to be speaking to humanity in the Bible with two voices: law and gospel. These voices are to be carefully distinguished, although never separated, in the process of biblical interpretation. It is important to make clear that the law-gospel distinction should not be equated with the difference between the Old and New Testaments. For Luther, both law and gospel are communicated in each testament, gospel in the Old as well as law in the New. Luther wrote about the character of the Old Testament: "Here you will find the swaddling cloths and the manger in which Christ lies, and to which the angel points the shepherds [Luke 2:12]. Simple and lowly are these swaddling cloths, but dear is the treasure, Christ, who lies in them."[18] While the New Testament has the gospel as its most authentic content, law and gospel are communicated in both testaments.

When we interpret Scripture as law and gospel, we turn our attention away from the literal text of the Bible and focus instead on the message being communicated. When the Word functions as law, it strikes the hearer as "demand," the demand to think in a certain way or to perform certain actions, in order to fulfill either human expectations or divine righteousness. The Word of God as law leaves the hearer to rely on one's own resources in satisfying whatever is required. According to the "first use" of the law, the requirements have to do with what society expects of us—as members of a family, workers at our jobs, citizens of a country, and members of the church. According to the "second use" of the law, the requirements have to do with what God expects of us, the fulfillment of the divine law, particularly as summarized in the Ten Commandments. On the one hand, confronted by God's requirements for our lives according to the second use of the law, we always fall short of fulfilling God's demands. On the other hand, while the human being has some capacity to fulfill society's expectations according to the first use of the law, we also fall short of completing all that is expected of us. This situation led Luther to the conclusion that "the law always accuses."[19] By our own effort and works, we always fail to satisfy the letter of the law. Accordingly, the spiritual function of the law convinces us of our sinfulness and prepares us to receive the gospel of Jesus Christ.

If the law places our lives under a demand, the character of the gospel extends God's unconditional promise.[20] In Jesus Christ, God speaks a Word of irrevocable grace, pardon, and hope: "Christ died for you!" "Your sins are forgiven!" "For Christ's sake you will inherit eternal life!" The Scripture is replete with texts that communicate this good news. For Luther, the ultimate purpose of the Bible is fulfilled only when it serves as the vehicle for the proclamation of the gospel. This means that the Bible itself is the Word of God only in an instrumental sense. Above all, the Word of God refers to Jesus Christ himself and to the living presence of Christ in the proclaimed gospel.[21] The Bible serves as a means of grace for bringing this Word of God to us, the gospel of Jesus Christ. Luther's view of law and gospel is well described by Prenter:

> Luther's view of Scripture can therefore be summarized thus: the Word as letter is law. As the letter it simply places us before a history which can only call us to be imitators. As the letter it places us alone on our own resources. As preaching, however, the Word is gospel. In the form of preaching the Word is a promise of the coming of the Spirit of God and his work in us.[22]

The Bible serves as a means for the living proclamation of the Word. The Holy Spirit finally determines how the hearer of the Word receives the biblical message, whether as law or as gospel. The same message might be heard by one person as law and received as gospel by another.

Lutheran interpretation of the Bible must continue to appropriate this foundational insight from Luther about law and gospel. The task of interpretation is not accomplished merely by undertaking scholarly exegesis, as indispensable as that may be. Rather, biblical scholarship must be put in service of the proclamation of God's Word by the church. Those who teach and preach the Bible in the Lutheran tradition must be attuned to the performance of Scripture as law and gospel. Finally, for Luther, only when the Bible is proclaimed as law and gospel does it become the living Word of God again for us.

Christ the Center (*Was Christum treibet*)

John 1:1–4 says, "In the beginning was the Word, and the Word was with God, and the Word was God. He was in the beginning with God. All things came into being through him, and without him not one thing came into being. What has come into being in him was life, and the life was the light of all people." As Luther interpreted God's Word, Jesus Christ served as his lens. Jesus Christ is the Word of God in its primary meaning. The witness of Scripture finally serves the proclamation of the crucified and risen Jesus Christ. As we interpret the Bible, Luther would have us acknowledge that Christ, who gives significance to the whole, is the center of Scripture. Ritva H. Williams writes,

> In his "Theses concerning Faith and Law" (1535) Luther even went so far as to declare that biblical texts must either refer to Christ or "must not be held to be true Scriptures." He consistently used the criterion of *was Christum treibet* ("whatever preaches Christ") to determine the relative status of the biblical texts.[23]

Luther employed the centrality of the message about Christ as a criterion for measuring the relative value of the different voices within Scripture. Based on their witness to Christ, Luther deemed the books of James and Revelation to be of lesser importance and perhaps not worthy of inclusion in the New Testament at all![24]

One way to distinguish among different ecumenical traditions within the whole of Christianity is by attending to their interpretation of Scripture. Various Christian churches find the warrant for their central convictions from different voices within the Bible.[25] Roman Catholics emphasize the role of Saint Peter as the primate to whom was entrusted authority in the church. Reformed traditions stress divine sovereignty in election and the Christian life lived to the glory of God. Methodists accent the sanctified life lived in response to God's grace, and Pentecostals focus on the gifts of the Holy Spirit manifest in the life of believers and the Christian community. The Lutheran tradition, by contrast, has placed primary focus on those biblical passages that testify to the justification of sinners by God's grace through faith in Jesus Christ alone: *Solus Christus!* While the Bible is authoritative in each denomination, where a particular tradition places the main accent within the whole counsel of Scripture becomes the basis for denominational distinctiveness. In significant ways, the differences between Christian denominations can be understood as contrasting claims about what is at the center of the Bible's message.[26]

The Lutheran movement might be considered a proposal to the whole Christian church about what should be considered the center of Scripture: the doctrine of justification by grace through faith in Jesus Christ alone.[27] The centrality of the gospel of Jesus Christ in the Bible is sometimes referred to as the Lutheran "canon within the canon." This means that in the interpretation of Scripture, the Lutheran Confessions give priority to the message of the gospel. While matters of the law (first or second use) have great significance for life in the world, these matters always remain "penultimate."[28] The "ultimate" truth of Scripture is that we are justified by grace through faith in Jesus Christ alone. Lutherans claim "Christ alone" as the Bible's central teaching. Texts that function as prescriptions of law are to be taken with great seriousness by the church. But finally, texts of legal significance are secondary to the message about the justifying grace of God in Jesus Christ. This is not antinomianism. It is to properly distinguish law and gospel.[29] The penultimate law always is located in relationship to the ultimate message of the gospel, God's justifying grace in Jesus Christ.

The Proper Use of Reason (*Vernunft*)

According to Luther, "Reason is the devil's greatest whore."[30] This may be the most famous quote of Luther on the significance of reason. Richard Dawkins and other great despisers of religion have made use of this sentiment to discredit religious belief.[31] However, taking this quote out of context distorts Luther's understanding of human reason. Just as Luther distinguished between two uses of the law, it is necessary also to distinguish between his two "uses" of reason. When Luther wrote his diatribe against Erasmus lambasting free will and reason, he was referring to their use *in cooperating to achieve salvation* (matters of the right-hand kingdom). Against such use of reason, Luther shouted protest. Only Jesus Christ works salvation! Neither works nor free will nor reason has any place here! By contrast, in the civic realm (or the left-hand kingdom), reason is one of the most excellent gifts of God to humanity, according to Luther. When considering matters of the created realm (not the realm of salvation), we employ reason to analyze and understand the world in the best possible way. For this reason, Luther was a staunch proponent of the value of education; the Lutheran church, following him, has been one of the leaders in supporting public education and establishing institutions of higher education.

The form of reasoning appropriate to the interpretation of the Bible is called hermeneutics.[32] Hermeneutics refers to the art of interpreting texts. In reflecting on the interpretive process, one useful construct is the "hermeneutical circle."[33] (See figure 1.) In the process of biblical interpretation, the hermeneutical circle begins with the assertion that God has spoken something to somebody through the words of a particular text of Scripture. In pursuit of the literal sense of this passage, the interpreter must attend to multiple aspects: the text itself (including attention to author, language, possible oral traditions, redactions), the audience (including attention to social location, time, place), the occasion of writing (including attention to purpose, rhetoric), and the world of the text (including attention to cultural milieu, religious environment, history). Employing as many exegetical methods of interpretation as the peculiarities of the text warrant, the interpreter arrives at some conclusions about its literal sense—that is, how the text functioned in the life of the earliest community to which it was directed. In the life of the church, these conclusions serve as the foundation for the proclamation of the text, just as the literal sense serves normatively in interpreting the meaning of the text.

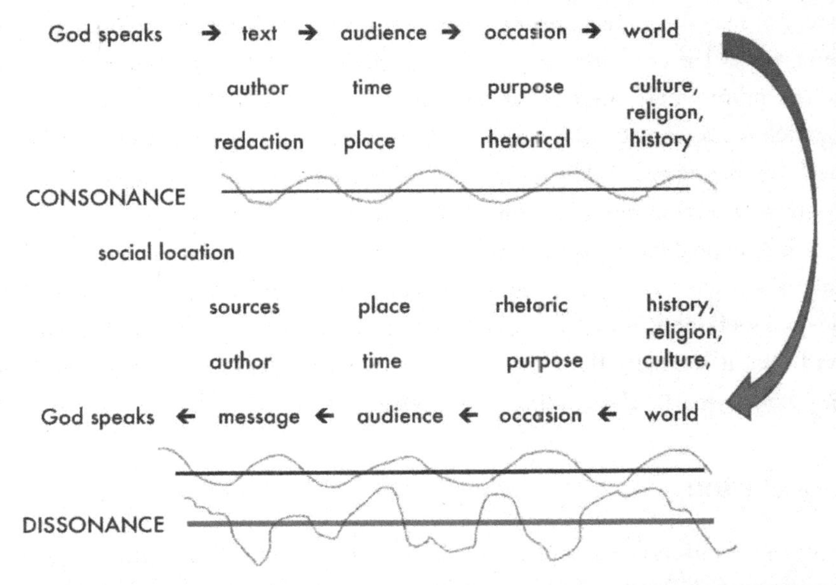

Figure 1. The hermeneutical circle
© 2009 Craig L. Nessan

For Lutherans, however, interpreting the Bible does not conclude with the first half of the hermeneutical circle. Biblical texts are for proclamation![34] The completion of the circle entails close attention to the context in which the text is claimed to be authoritative now: the world of the interpreter (including attention to culture, religious environment, history), the occasion (including attention to purpose, rhetoric), the audience (including attention to social location, time, place), and message (including attention to author/interpreter, language, sources).[35] As an outcome of interpretation, the interpreter dares to believe that God once again speaks through the text, both law and gospel.

How does one evaluate the legitimacy of interpretation, given the complexities of the hermeneutical process? The aim of interpretation is to create *consonance* between the literal sense of the text and the claims for significance to the present hearers. In a consonant performance of the text, there is recognizable congruity between its speaking to the earliest community to whom it was directed and speaking of the text to a specific community today. While the two performances are not identical, the interpreter can render accounts for inevitable *dissonance* between the literal sense of the text and the claims about its meaning in the present. In some cases, the very acknowledgment of the dissonance may preserve a greater sense of consonance. There are occasions, however, where the contemporary performance of the biblical text may degenerate to the point where there is virtually no correspondence with its literal sense. In such instances, the dissonance is so pervasive that we can only describe the performance as failed. The hermeneutical circle has broken down, and one must begin with a fresh interpretation of the text.

Hermeneutical reasoning is a complex activity, analogous more to an art than a science. Such reasoning is indispensable to the process of interpretation, despite its fallibility. As we shall yet see in the next chapter on the authority of tradition, it is finally the faith community that renders a verdict on the legitimacy of any particular reading of Scripture.

Conclusion

Every generation faces controversy about the proper interpretation and proclamation of Scripture. Today such debates are complicated both by literalist claims and by postmodern sensibilities. Literalists claim that Scripture must be interpreted so that each verse supports an established theological framework.[36]

In this system, the Bible serves to substantiate fixed doctrinal assertions about God and the world. Metaphor becomes proof. The central purpose of the Bible is to provide the truths (propositional revelation) needed to understand God correctly and live our lives obediently. Due to the prominence of this approach to biblical interpretation, especially in the media, it has influenced many people—including many Lutherans. This poses a major challenge for teachers and pastors in the Lutheran tradition: to present a credible alternative to literalist and fundamentalist interpretation. How do we undertake the immense challenge of teaching and preaching the Bible with integrity, given the influence of literalist approaches?

A completely different but challenging undertaking involves our engagement with postmodern approaches, many of which grant the Bible no special status or authority. Within a postmodern sensibility, there is resistance to all normative readings of the Bible as Scripture. Each interpreter claims personal authority to read the Bible idiosyncratically: "This is what it means to me." In the postmodern context, the Bible has many meanings, depending on my own perspective or that of my subculture. All readings exist side by side, with none daring to claim anything approaching universal validity. While this postmodern situation promotes the virtue of tolerance toward difference, it undermines every claim to the "truth" of Scripture for the life and mission of the church. If in the case of literalism, the meaning of Scripture is zealously overdetermined, in many postmodern readings it is woefully underdetermined.

A Lutheran approach to the interpretation of Scripture for our time must navigate a course between the tsunami of literalism and the undertow of postmodernity. This chapter proposed six theological affirmations for a distinctively Lutheran approach to biblical interpretation: God speaks, finite human words bear the infinite Word of God, privileging of the literal sense, attending to how Scripture functions as law and gospel, Christ as the center of the biblical message, and the proper use of hermeneutical reasoning. This theological framework can guide the church in appealing with integrity to the authority of Scripture for ethics. The Evangelical Lutheran Church in America's Constitution states the following about the nature of Scripture:

> The canonical Scriptures of the Old and New Testaments are the written Word of God. Inspired by God's Spirit speaking through their authors, they record and announce God's revelation centering in Jesus Christ.

> Through them God's Spirit speaks to us to create and sustain Christian faith and fellowship for service in the world.[37]

These Lutheran insights about the interpretation of Scripture can guide the church through tempestuous times, lending confidence in God's providence as God speaks the Word we need to hear in our time.

2 The Authority of Tradition, Reason, and Experience

WHILE THE HOLY SCRIPTURE TAKES FIRST and central place as authority for faith and life, theology and ethics, this chapter will reflect on the contributions of three other classical sources of authority: tradition, reason, and experience. Taken together, these four compose what is sometimes referred to as the "Wesley Quadrilateral," although all four sources of authority have been prevalent in every Christian generation and predate John Wesley (1703–91).[1]

The Authority of Tradition

Tradition, in Lutheran perspective, especially relates to trajectories of meaning launched from Scripture and how authority has been contested through historical struggle and articulated in classic formulations: canon, creeds, councils, doctrines, and confessions. We examine two core themes related to tradition in relationship to the authority of the Bible: (1) that God continues to speak through Scripture with a living voice and (2) that the interpretation of biblical texts is inexorably a contest among competing claims in need of resolution.

Living Voice of God (*Viva vox Dei*)

Isaiah 55:10–11 says, "For as the rain and the snow come down from heaven, and do not return there until they have watered the earth, making it bring forth and sprout, giving seed to the sower and bread to the eater, so shall my word be that goes out from my mouth; it shall not return to me empty, but it shall accomplish that which I purpose, and succeed in the thing for which I sent it." The Word of God is dynamic in speaking throughout the ages. We are not the first generation to have attended to God's voice through Scripture. Beginning with the earliest church, listeners in every new context have heard God speaking in their own time and place. This is the Spirit's work, to bring the Bible to life so that God's Word speaks anew in every generation.

A fruitful concept from hermeneutical theory is that texts possess a "surplus of meaning."[2] The significance of a given text is not exhausted by how it functioned in the earliest community to which it was directed (as discussed in the previous chapter). Instead, especially for Scripture, the biblical text becomes the living voice of God in ever-new contexts of interpretation, where it functions again and again as Word of God for new hearers. Over time, Bible texts continue to mean new things to new people in new settings.

The proposition that biblical texts have a surplus of meaning entails that they invite new and fresh interpretations in ever-emerging contexts. For example, consider how Augustine in the fourth century, Martin Luther at the time of the Reformation, and preachers of every generation, including now, have differently interpreted the same biblical texts for their contemporaries, yet with inspired meaning. Dare we claim that every new interpretation adds a new layer of meaning to the text? This is truly the destiny of biblical texts as they are interpreted over time. Every new interpreter in every new context adds another layer to the tradition of interpretation. (See figure 2.)

As we understand Scripture as God's living voice in ever-new contexts and generations, it boggles the mind to imagine the diversity of possible interpretations and proclamations that have been offered for the same text. We have in chapter 1 contended that the "literal sense" of the text has normative significance for the process of interpretation. Yet, as preachers know, the interpretation of Scripture for sermons is no mere reiteration of the literal sense. Rather, every new rendering is carried out in its own hermeneutical setting (including world situation, occasion, audience, and message) that leads to the disclosure of new significance.

A flood of questions emerges: How does one discern whether a new interpretation is legitimate? Are there interpretations to be rejected? On what basis would one determine the difference between a legitimate and an illegitimate reading? Postmodern sensibilities are troubled by such questions. Radical reader-response criticism, for example, affirms an infinite number of readings, none of which should be deemed more or less legitimate. Deconstruction becomes wary of all attempts to impose authority over the process of interpretation. The claim that there are legitimate and illegitimate readings finds itself in acute tension

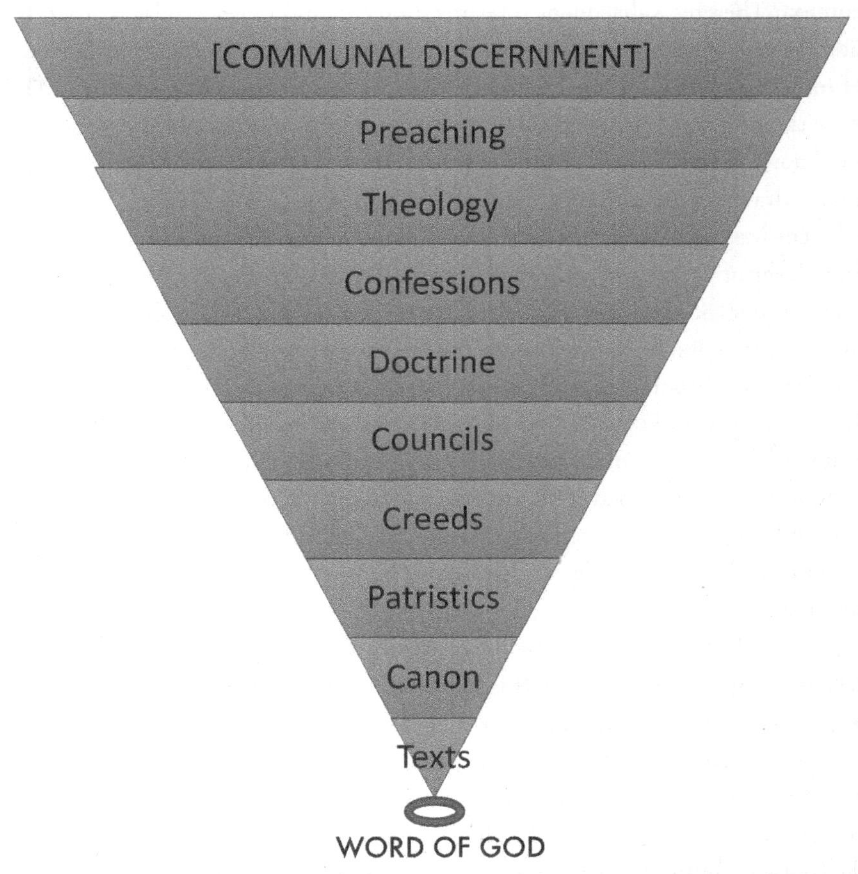

Figure 2. The traditioning process
© 2009 Craig L. Nessan

with postmodern interpreters who argue that no interpretation deserves norma-tive significance, lest it become the basis for oppression and control.

Among the people of God, however, the interpretation of the Bible has always been understood as part of the church's "traditioning process." The original speaking of the text, how it functioned in the earliest community to which it was first directed, serves as the norm for all subsequent interpreta-tion. Later interpreters are challenged to seek consonance between the meaning of the text in its original speaking and the speaking of the text in their own context. Thereby, subsequent interpretations should never say "less" than the literal sense of the text. The literal sense should not be contradicted by later acts of interpretation. However, according to the surplus of meaning by which texts have the power to transcend their original speaking, it is possible for the text to say "more" than it had ever previously said. Each text has a reservoir of meaning that is drawn on in each new act of interpretation.

The history of interpretation, like sheets of sedimentary stone, is composed from layer upon layer of meanings deposited over time. One of the most consequential decisions for the history of interpretation was the establishing of the biblical canon itself. As we know from the vast array of apocryphal writings in the earliest Christian centuries, there was not always agreement about which were to be the authoritative writings. Prior to the establishment of the canon, many other texts circulated with their own claims to authority. Eventually, the canonical texts emerged with authority as God's Word and became the normative basis for the church's proclamation. Had other writings been deemed canonical, the traditioning process, as we know it, might have run a quite different course.

Once deemed canonical, each Scripture text has its own history of interpretation, vastly complex. Within this history, certain readings have become classic (e.g., those by the church fathers, saints, doctors, and reformers of the church). Classical readings are those that warrant serious engagement by later interpreters.[3] Other readings have been declared normative, especially at times of acute controversy in the history of the church (e.g., the formulation of the creeds, the decisions of councils, or the forging of confessions). Such normative readings have been established by the church to regulate all subsequent interpretations.[4] Still other readings have been judged deficient, distorted, misleading, or even dangerous. These readings have been excluded by the church in the traditioning process and in some cases even declared heretical.

Each generation is faced with the challenge of interpreting Scripture authentically in its own time and place. Interpreters are challenged to create consonance between the speaking of the text as it functioned for the earliest community to which it was directed and the present hermeneutical context. Every new interpretation is added as another layer to the traditioning process. Moreover, in every generation, there emerges a contest to distinguish legitimate from illegitimate readings.[5] To discern the Word of God amid all the human words is a communal task of the church in every generation.

The Contest of Interpretations

One of the perennial questions facing the church in its interpretation of Scripture is how to negotiate among competing claims within the Bible itself. For example, based on the same Bible, some claim it legitimate to employ violence to resolve conflict, while others only allow for nonviolent measures. From the same authoritative Scripture, some hold it necessary to be "born again" through a decision for Christ, while others hold infant baptism to be a legitimate path to salvation. From the authority of the same Word of God, some make predictions about those things to occur in the end times, while others hold that no one knows either the day or the hour of Christ's return. There are plenteous instances of how those committed to biblical authority wrangle with one another in making competing claims about what the Bible really says and means.

The Lutheran Confessional tradition can be understood as a proposal to the whole Christian church about what should be considered the center of Scripture: the doctrine of justification by grace through faith in Jesus Christ alone. (See figure 3.) Lutherans give priority to the gospel in the interpretation of biblical texts. As Lutherans enter the arena of contested interpretations, they bring to the deliberation what is central to the Lutheran Confession, insistence on Jesus Christ and the gospel as the most significant focus. This does not mean inattention to the literal sense of biblical texts. But it does mean focused theological attention on what Lutherans confess as the center of the whole counsel of Scripture, the gospel of Jesus Christ.

Other Christian traditions bring their own claims about what is most central in Scripture to this contest of interpretations. One of the most provocative proposals in recent times comes from locations of extreme poverty and injustice. Out of the context of the poor in Latin America, the suffering ones in Africa, the Dalits in India, or the oppressed African American community in the US, the question has been posed, Is there not overwhelming testimony about God's concern for justice at the heart of Scripture? This is nothing less than a dramatic proposal to the whole church about another canon within the canon. If Lutherans propose that the gospel with its *justification trajectory* is a canon within the canon of Scripture, the churches of the impoverished world ask whether there is not also a *justice trajectory* within Scripture that we must heed.[6] This justice trajectory began with God hearing the cries of the slaves in Egypt, continued with the exodus, became encoded in the laws of Israel in defense of the poor, established expectations for kings to do justice, and was ignited in the words of

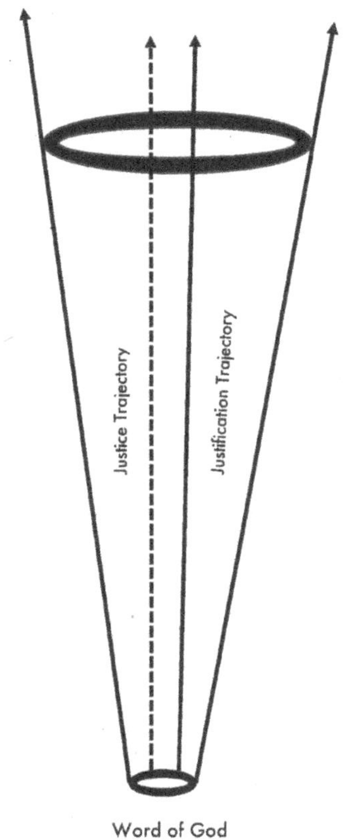

Figure 3. Canon within a canon
© 2009 Craig L. Nessan

the prophets. It concludes with Jesus's own concern for the dawning of God's just and peaceable kingdom expressed in his teaching, practice, cross, and resurrection. As Lutherans propose that Scripture is centered on God's saving grace in Jesus Christ, how do we respond to the proposal that there is a justice trajectory that is core to the Holy Bible?

Finally, it falls to the church to deliberate which readings of Scripture are consonant with the literal sense, which are marginal readings, and even which are excluded readings. (See figure 4.) This process within the church can be and usually is tempestuous. It is a process that the members of the church need

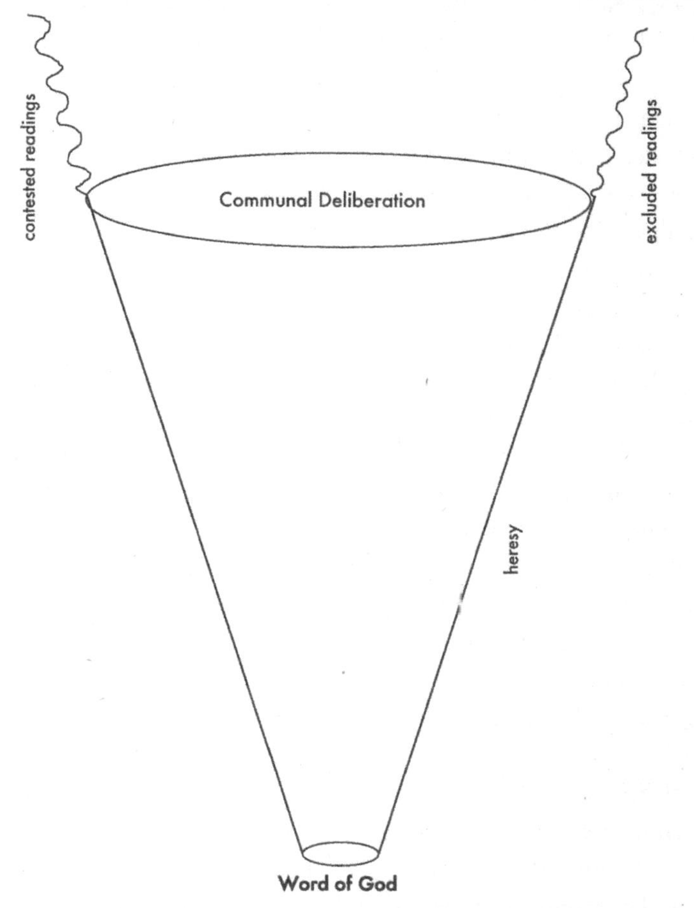

Figure 4. Communal deliberation
© 2009 Craig L. Nessan

to enter in a spirit of prayerfulness. Every generation engages in its own contests over the authority and meaning of Scripture. The Reformation itself was in many ways a contest over the proper interpretation of Scripture: Were Luther and the other reformers correct in their theological claim that the gospel of grace in Jesus Christ is the central message of the Bible upon which to implement reforms? More recent generations have battled over matters such as the legitimacy of slavery or the status of women in the life of the church, arguing over how to read Scripture on these questions. Today one intense contest rages over what the Bible says about homosexuality and the place of gay and lesbian persons in the church. One of the great complications in this contest involves conflicting paradigms employed to interpret the pertinent Bible passages.[7] How does a church that affirms Scripture as the final norm for the church's faith and life negotiate conflicting interpretations of the Bible itself? This is a contemporary example of what is at stake as the church engages in communal deliberation over the interpretation of Scripture today.

We who are the church in this generation are called upon to enter the fray of contested interpretations with integrity and charity, employing our best exegetical skills and wisdom to understand the literal sense of biblical texts and to create consonance between that literal sense and the proclamation needed in our own context. We are responsible for the new layers of meaning added to the tradition of interpretation in our time. We are called upon to participate in the communal process of negotiating which interpretations are considered legitimate and which are precluded. We are summoned to pray for the Spirit's guidance as we seek to remain faithful to God's living Word in our time.

Where the church has arrived at decisions based on communal deliberation as formulated in creeds, conciliar decisions, doctrines, confessions, or contemporary denominational resolutions, these become essential to the ongoing interpretive process. Because the church arrived at authoritative interpretations of Scripture at definitive moments in the past, often during times of controversy, these readings have become part of the normative tradition and belong to the inheritance of later generations for discerning how to render faithfully the meaning of God's Word in our time. This is an extraordinarily complex process. The churches, as they are organized into deliberative bodies, bear responsibility for negotiating how Scripture should exercise authority today among those who belong to their membership. The ongoing ecumenical task involves how families of churches reconcile themselves in their differences and move toward affirmation of one another's teachings, ethical practices, and order. The goal of the ecumenical process is mutual recognition of one another's ministries on the way to full communion within the body of Christ. Jesus prays, "I ask not only on behalf of these, but also on behalf of those who will believe in me through their word, that they may all be one. As you, Father, are in me and I am in you, may they also be in us, so that the world may believe that you have sent me" (John 17:20–21).

The Authority of Reason

Especially since the Enlightenment, reason has been valued as the central, if not primary, source for human decision-making. However, with the rise of the postmodern, the authority of reason has been called into radical question by interpretive methods, such as deconstruction, that seek to unmask the subjectivity and self-interest of the truth claims of every author. Epistemologically, the postmodern condition is marked by subjectivism and relativism. No credence is given to all-encompassing metanarratives.[8] Truth is understood as relative to the author. "My" truth may be different from "your" truth. Truth claims are understood as socially constructed.[9] This key feature of the postmodern can easily morph into hyperindividualism. According to hyperindividualism, every individual operates with a sense of individual autonomy in relation to the truth claims of others, even of consensus viewpoints in the sciences and social sciences.

There are signs that the postmodern has transformed into what might be called the "posttruth" era.[10] In our age, we are losing all sense of direction for shared meaning. Public discourse is constructed, even manipulated, to serve narrow political self-interests. New versions of "truth" are invented hour by hour and day by day to suit ambition. The common ground for constructing the foundations of a good society becomes questionable and easily doubted. The willingness to negotiate truth claims is allowable only with those who share your own political agenda. Civil society is impossible, however, without mutual commitment to pursue the common good beyond partisanship. Democracy is possible only through an exercise of goodwill that is willing to acknowledge a measure of truth in the arguments of others. In a time when all truths have become contested, it is imperative to reclaim the value of human reason as a source of authority for ethical deliberation.

Philosophically, the definition of reason is complicated, differentiating itself from other mental faculties, such as sensation, emotion, or will. An operative definition of reason in ethics holds that reason involves the ability to gather available and reliable information in a process that carefully evaluates this evidence in drawing a conclusion. Every conclusion is preliminary and subject to revision based on new data. The reasoning process in ethical deliberation gains strength by drawing upon reliable information from science, social science, and the humanities in arriving at conclusions based on the wisdom from each of these fields.

While we will focus attention on the value of the sciences for ethics, literature and the arts are bearers of truth that inform and deepen ethical reflection. The most subtle and complex of human truths have been conveyed through the classics, whether in literature, poetry, music, painting, sculpture, or other artistic forms. David Tracy writes,

> The classics of any culture have always functioned culturally as phenomena in the public realm of a particular culture through their disclosive and transformative shareable possibilities. Those possibilities come to us through the more elusive, but no less real, form of inquiry as conversation with classic texts, persons, symbols, rituals, and so forth than through the more usual form of argument. . . . Classics usually appeal first to the imagination, not to argument or personal preference. But once the possibilities of the disclosive vision in the classic are acknowledged as possibilities in the present, they come to us as candidates for some new consensus on possibility itself for the entire community of inquiry—candidates that now function with the public impact of a truth as disclosure, not truth as the result of an explicit conclusion of an argument.[11]

These sources of authority from the humanities have compelling value for ethical formation and action.

Formal reasoning aims to think coherently and draw logical inferences and conclusions from facts assumed to be true. The reasoning process begins with testing data and evidence based on careful observation in a process of evaluating this information in arriving at conclusions. Reason is challenged wherever there is a contest about what constitutes "reliable" data, something that today often appears nearly irresolvable in competition with those who refuse to allow informed agreement about facts. The reasoning process becomes clouded by disputes over the factual basis of truth claims and how to value the significance of certain facts in relation to others.

Amid the disintegration of reasoning in this era of posttruth, use of the scientific method can inform ethics through the method of "critical realism." Ian Barbour views critical realism as "an alternative to three competing interpretations of scientific theories: (1) classical or naïve realism: scientific theories provide a 'photographic' or literal representation of the world; (2) instrumentalism: scientific theories are mere calculative devices, and (3) idealism: scientific theories depict reality as mental."[12] Critical realism aims at ever-greater approximations of truth by employing reason as a key source of authority. While language can never fully correspond to the fullness of reality, some explanations, based on scientific reasoning, provide better approximations of reality than others; by contrast, other explanations are totally inaccurate or even aim to deceive.

Scientific method involves the formulation of hypotheses, isolation of variables, and performing experiments to gather data and draw conclusions based on the findings. It is of great value to pay attention to consensus positions in the sciences as a source of authority when undertaking ethical deliberation, also in the church. The fruitfulness of scientific reasoning has been demonstrated by its achievements in every arena of human investigation—for example, medicine, genetics, agriculture, or meteorology. The social sciences—such as psychology, sociology, political science, or economics—are fields of inquiry also strengthened by conformation to the standards of scientific inquiry.

Theological ethics must take into consideration three possible limits to reason as a source of authority. First, as we have seen, postmodernism exercises skepticism about the legitimacy of the reasoning process in arriving at universally valid conclusions. This necessitates the need to defend the validity of scientific consensus undergirding the use of reasoning in theological argument. Second, scientific findings can be and have been employed for immoral purposes. For example, it is imperative to examine the values that inform specific research agendas and their application of scientific findings to promote projects that harm human life and creation itself. Third, reason has an absolute limit in attaining direct access to transcendent reality. Transcendent reality is mediated by human claims about divine experience. This is also true for claims to mystical experience. The method of critical realism, therefore, has implications also for theological ethics as competing truth claims are tested through a theology of the religions.[13]

The classic statement of the relationship between theological truth and reason was formulated by Anselm as "faith seeking understanding." Faith is not contrary to reason but has its origin in God, who is the author both of what has been revealed religiously and of what has been discovered through human reasoning. Pope Francis writes,

> In a pluralistic society, dialogue is the best way to realize what ought always to be affirmed and respected apart from any ephemeral consensus.

> Such dialogue needs to be enriched and illumined by clear thinking, rational arguments, a variety of perspectives, and the contribution of different fields of knowledge and points of view. Nor can it exclude the conviction that it is possible to arrive at certain fundamental truths always to be upheld. Acknowledging the existence of certain enduring values, however demanding it may be to discern them, makes for a robust and solid social ethics. Once those fundamental values are acknowledged and adopted through dialogue and consensus, we realize that they rise above consensus; they transcend our concrete situations and remain non-negotiable. Our understanding of their meaning and scope can increase—and in that respect, consensus is a dynamic reality—but in themselves, they are held to be enduring by virtue of their inherent meaning.[14]

According to this approach, all truth is ultimately grounded in God. Because all truth has divine origin, this leads to the supposition that finally all truth is unified through the workings of the divine Creator. Therefore, people of faith have nothing to fear by incorporating scientific information into their worldview. Faith will be strengthened, not undermined, by an alignment with all other sources of truth. As scientific paradigms shift, it becomes the ever-new task of theology to expand its understanding to incorporate new discoveries, especially those based on scientific consensus. What we know about God becomes ever more expansive through attention paid to the sources of human knowledge about the world God has created. Reason thus has a crucial role to play as an ongoing source of authority for theology.

The Authority of Experience

Claims to the authority of experience are highly complex and can often be highly debatable. Philosophical interpretation of human experience encompasses not only ordinary waking experience but exploration of brain processes, dream states, and atypical human states of consciousness. A commonsense working definition might describe experience as a living perception of events. Experience entails a personal perception or observation of events as they occur, an existential encounter with a set of circumstances in the world.

One thing is clear: human beings are deeply committed to the authenticity of their own experiences. This means it is extremely difficult to dispute or refute claims to the authority of experience by other people. Moreover, in considering the experiences of others, we note how the range of experience varies dramatically from person to person. While some persons have a vast array of experiences from encounters with other people and learning from many varied contexts, other people have a fairly limited range of experiences based on their daily routines and relationships within a defined locale.

People also employ different language, especially contrasting metaphors, and interpretive frameworks to describe their experiences. As one can imagine based on witness testimony at court, the same event can be experienced and interpreted very differently by those who were present at the same occurrence. This involves myriad factors, including selective attention to details, filtering the event through one's own previous experiences, and the use of contrasting explanatory frameworks. One literary example of the influence of subjective interpretation is based on the folktale from India "The Blind Men and the Elephant":

> The first blind man reached out and touched the side of the huge animal. "An elephant is smooth and solid like a wall!" he declared. "It must be very powerful."
>
> The second blind man put his hand on the elephant's limber trunk. "An elephant is like a giant snake," he announced.
>
> The third blind man felt the elephant's pointed tusk. "I was right," he decided. "This creature is as sharp and deadly as a spear."
>
> The fourth blind man touched one of the elephant's four legs. "What we have here," he said, "is an extremely large cow."
>
> The fifth blind man felt the elephant's giant ear. "I believe an elephant is like a huge fan or maybe a magic carpet that can fly over mountains and treetops," he said.
>
> The sixth blind man gave a tug on the elephant's coarse tail. "Why, this is nothing more than a piece of old rope. Dangerous, indeed," he scoffed.[15]

This story well illustrates the subjectivity of experience and how we as humans can become very attached to the truth of our own perceptions.

In order to enhance the validity of experience as a source of authority, it is vital that we intentionally listen to and learn from the experiences of others. This means expanding the range of our own experience by encountering the life-changing experiences of other people. We are purposely able to cultivate a broader range of experience in our own lives and in the lives of others through our interactions with them. Education is one crucial resource for broadening one's range of experience. Education tests our operative categories for interpreting experience and expands our capacity to imagine different ways of thinking about our experiences. Moreover, we can intentionally place ourselves in situations that challenge prior assumptions and lead us to rethink them. For example, engaging in cross-cultural immersions or encounters with people from different contexts can have profound effects on how one's experience is transformed.

As we think about the place of human experience as an authority for ethical deliberation, it is imperative that claims to experience be tested in relation to the other three standards of authority:

1. Does one's experience conform to the witness of Scripture, especially to the two central trajectories of justification and justice?
2. Does one's experience conform to the witness of tradition, especially to the central witnesses of the historic creeds, confessions, and doctrines of the church?
3. Does one's experience conform to reason, especially to consensus positions in the sciences, social sciences, and humanities?
4. Does one's experience conform to shared human experience as it would be commonly interpreted by other people?

Of the four sources of theological authority employed in ethical deliberation, this discussion concludes that experience is the least stable. Although many people may be very attached to their experiences as a source for making decisions, one's personal experience needs to be checked by warrants from Scripture, tradition, reason, and shared human experience as a source of authority for ethics.

Conclusion

The first two chapters have explored the primary sources of authority for Lutheran ethics, first through an exploration of the themes that inform a Lutheran hermeneutic to interpret Scripture: (1) God speaks a living word through biblical texts; (2) finite texts are the bearer of the infinite Word of God; (3) we are to privilege the literal sense of God's Word, understood as the meaning of texts to their original hearers; (4) God's Word functions as law and gospel; (5) Christ is the center of the biblical message; and (6) we value engaging in hermeneutical reasoning.

Chapter 2 has discussed how Scripture functions to create a living tradition based on the surplus of meaning inherent in biblical texts. The traditioning process must be negotiated over time by the church according to a contest of interpretations to determine how texts are to function authoritatively within diverse contexts, according to new insights from other intellectual disciplines, and in relationship to previous interpretation. In the ongoing contest of interpretations, there can be either continuity with or disruption from the conclusions of the Spirit. This chapter also has described some of the ways reason, especially reasoning based on scientific method, and human experience function as legitimate sources of authority for theological ethics as well as described some of the limitations of these sources of authority. In chapter 3, we turn next to a discussion of the meaning of "gospel freedom" in contrast to the conventional meanings of freedom embedded in the American context. It is imperative that we gain clarity on the specificity of Christian freedom, lest we be confused by the prevailing notions of freedom in contemporary society.

3 Gospel Freedom in American Context

ONE OF THE MOST MISUNDERSTOOD THEOLOGICAL words in the American context is *freedom*. It is almost certainly the case that when a pastor reads the word *freedom* from the Bible or discusses it in preaching and teaching that the majority of listeners will misconstrue its meaning. This is a consequence of the overwhelming influence of distinctively "American" meanings that locate freedom in relation to lifestyle, political, economic, or military realms. While such understandings of freedom have their proper place, the connotations derived from American society and public life have little direct connection to the distinctive character of Christian freedom. This chapter first explores the conventional meanings of freedom in American society. Second, we examine the meaning of freedom in the work of David Foster Wallace, whose interpretation of freedom can build a bridge to Christian theology. Third, we elaborate on the unique meaning of freedom in the theology of Martin Luther and its crucial significance for Lutheran ethics. Finally, we circle back to connect American meanings of freedom to theological interpretation.

Freedom in American Context

If there is a single word that characterizes the conventional understanding of what it means to be American, it is *freedom.* This corresponds to the highly individualized construal of each person's right to choose what to think and how to live in American society.[1] Freedom means the right to say and do whatever I please, normally insofar as it does no physical harm to others. Individualism, or hyperindividualism, is one of the most distinguishable characteristics of

American society in contrast to other countries of the world. When visitors experience American society, they quickly notice the limited regard individuals have for the well-being of other people, let alone the common good. Freedom is about lifestyle choices, the right to self-expression in appearance, dress, behavior, and many other personal preferences regardless of what others may think. This is the primary meaning of freedom in daily life and experience.

This existential sense of freedom is grounded in political rights defined and protected constitutionally. These include freedom of religion, freedom of speech, and freedom of the press. These political privileges also include the basic right to peaceful assembly and the right to petition the government for redress of grievances. These five liberties are each named specifically in the First Amendment to the Constitution.[2] These political freedoms belong at the heart of American democracy. They distinguish the political arrangements that constitute the ideals to which America aspires, regardless of the many contradictions to these standards throughout American history and yet today.

While these First Amendment freedoms have been established by law, American history to this day has been desecrated by the contradictions to these ideals: genocides against Indigenous people and enslaved people; the long history of Jim Crow, lynching, and systemic racism; inequality for women in every life sphere; maltreatment of LGBTQIA+ persons; discrimination against Muslims and people of other faiths; denial of due process to asylum seekers and those seeking immigrant status; disregard for poor people; and many other violations against human dignity as measured by the founding documents. The claims about American freedom need always to be tested by the treatment of the most vulnerable, those being excluded from exercising their constitutional rights.[3] Claims of American superiority ring hollow in the face of those who have been left behind by the American dream.[4]

Closely related to these contradictions are those created by the inequalities in the American economic system, the third aspect to the meaning of freedom in America.[5] While defenders of American capitalism are devoted to the faith that this system is best equipped to provide for the welfare of all, the ideology has never been and is not now authenticated by reality. The premise of the American economic system is that hard work will be rewarded by success. The corollary of this premise is that those who are poor suffer due to their own failed effort. Furthermore, such failure is conventionally interpreted not only as a moral flaw but as a character defect. The consequence is that those who are trapped in generational cycles of poverty or those who have experienced difficult life circumstances that have led to economic hardship are blamed for their condition.

The stark truth is that economic success is largely a result of the life circumstances one has inherited as a privilege of birth. While there are instances of upward economic mobility from the lower and middle classes, often due to personal educational achievement or unique opportunities, these cases are cited publicly as the norm rather than the exception. This perpetuates the myth that American capitalism best serves the needs of all.[6] To the contrary, wealth in America is first of all the result of inheritance from previous generations. Families of great wealth perpetuate themselves from generation to generation. This is facilitated by tax laws that benefit the rich and by inheritance laws that fail to redistribute wealth at the time of death.

Moreover, the 2010 Citizens United ruling by the Supreme Court that designated corporations as persons and thereby served to eliminate limits on independent corporate spending during elections has greatly intensified the crisis we face in America.[7] Increasingly, public officials and representatives are more obligated to the corporations that financed their elections than to the common good of the country. This has created a crisis for safeguarding all the political freedoms designated in the US Constitution, as the privileges of wealth take precedence over all other factors in governance and lawmaking. The disregard for public opinion by elected officials has escalated dramatically as economic power continues to undermine the American society. The wealth gap between the top 1 percent and the rest of the population continues to widen with the free fall of the middle class into debt and accelerating poverty. At the same time, those trapped in poverty by circumstances of birth, systemic racism, and the transfer of wealth from the middle class to the superrich continues unabated.[8]

The final factor for consideration in this analysis of the conventional meaning of freedom involves the exercise of military force to defend and extend these American values globally. America has the largest military budget and most extensively deployed military operations in the world. The US military represents the guarantee placed upon American lifestyle, political, and economic freedoms. The rehearsal of American military victories in World War I, World War II, Korea, Vietnam, Iraq, Afghanistan, and the heroic status afforded those serving in the military demonstrates how this fourth meaning of freedom is fully integrated with the other three. American freedoms have been and continue to be worth defending through military action wherever necessary.[9]

The exercise of military force by the US is interpreted as necessary to protect democracy at home and to extend it throughout the world. Given the intertwining of lifestyle, political, and economic dimensions of American freedom, however, in recent decades, military action has especially been exercised to protect and extend the economic interests of corporate investments. For example, American corporate interests in accessing the production of oil have entangled foreign policy in Middle East conflicts for several decades. In previous decades, similar corporate interests contributed to military interventions in Central America. This has been a pattern marking military action throughout American history but increasingly after World War II. This has led to foreign policy lending military support to governments where America has economic interests, even when those countries do not support lifestyle or political freedoms.

Another ominous development is the increasing militarization of policing, not only at the borders, but especially in American cities. The war against drugs that began in the 1980s included the training and arming of local police forces to employ military tactics on the civil population, especially among African Americans, leading to the mass incarceration of people of color disproportionately for drug offenses.[10] This same trend toward domestic militarization after 9/11 led to the formation of the Department of Homeland Security in 2002, now the third-largest cabinet department in the US after the Departments of Defense and Veterans Affairs. The employment of Homeland Security forces has continued to expand beyond its original mandate to use military force in domestic affairs. Domestic militarization also has led not only to military conditions imposed by the US Border Patrol to control immigration across the Mexican border but to the deployment of those forces to control US citizens in cities far from international borders. The deployment of military forces against American citizens also endangers lifestyle and political freedoms.

The observance of national holidays, such as Memorial Day, Independence Day, and Veterans Day, integrates the three prior meanings of freedom together with that of the military. The four dimensions of American freedom—lifestyle, political, economic, and military—constitute a matrix that defines the conventional meaning of freedom in American society that is deeply embedded in the rituals and core beliefs of American civil religion.[11] We confess this freedom in the Pledge of Allegiance, sing this freedom in the National Anthem, and spend this freedom imprinted on our money. From this discussion, we have established the conventional meaning of freedom when the word is used in everyday life. This usage contrasts so greatly with the biblical and theological traditions that it is almost impossible to communicate the core meaning of Christian freedom among church members. We will next explore the exposition of freedom by David Foster Wallace, whose work can assist in bridging between American freedom and Christian freedom.

Human Freedom according to David Foster Wallace

The author David Foster Wallace can be a constructive interlocutor for a deeper analysis of the nature of human freedom in the American context. Foster Wallace was a brilliant young novelist and essayist whose most well-known book is entitled *Infinite Jest*.[12] His work has been acclaimed through critical studies not only in literary circles but among philosophers and theologians.[13] Here we draw attention to one brief but masterful analysis of the human condition first delivered by Foster Wallace as a commencement address at Kenyon College in 2005. The address is of significant interest for its concise and trenchant insights on the possibilities and limits of human freedom. The speech has been published as *This Is Water: Some Thoughts, Delivered on a Significant Occasion, about Living a Compassionate Life*, and the original talk is also available online.[14]

After his introductory remarks, Foster Wallace explores what it might mean to receive an education that involves "teaching you how to think." Quickly, he moves beyond what might be considered platitudes to focus not on thinking itself but on "the choice of what to think about."[15] What is most significant about thinking is the recognition that we make ethical choices not only in relation to what we say or do but precisely in what and how we choose to think about things. Foster Wallace says,

> The point here is that I think this is one part of what the liberal arts mantra of "teaching me how to think" is really supposed to mean: to be just a little less arrogant, to have some "critical awareness" about myself and my certainties . . . because a huge percentage of the stuff that I tend to be automatically certain of is, it turns out, totally wrong and deluded.[16]

How you decide to interpret what goes on around you in the world in daily life entails a crucial ethical decision.

This leads Foster Wallace to introduce a key term to his analysis of the human condition, our "default setting":

Everything in my own immediate experience supports my deep belief that I am the absolute center of the universe, the realest, most vivid and important person in existence. We rarely think about this sort of natural, basic self-centeredness, because it's so socially repulsive, but it's pretty much the same for all of us, deep down.[17]

This default setting, Foster Wallace claims, is "hardwired into our boards at birth." This leads to the assertion that each of us has been and remains always at the absolute center of every experience. The decision before us every moment is always between responding to others and the world by "choosing to do the work of somehow altering or getting free of my natural, hardwired default setting, which is to be deeply and literally self-centered, and to see and interpret everything through the lens of self."[18]

One danger of an academic education is that we learn to give more attention to our own intellectual life than to what might be the case going on in the world around us. "Learning to think" thus entails paying attention in exercising "some control over *how* and *what* you think."[19] To the graduates, Foster Wallace poses this challenge:

How to keep from going through your comfortable, prosperous, respectable adult life dead, unconscious, a slave to your head and to your natural default setting of being uniquely, completely, imperially alone, day in and day out.[20]

He proceeds to describe how the greater part of daily life for human beings always involves tedium, routine, and causes for distress.

Foster Wallace gives an object lesson in what the challenges of ordinary life really entail. He invites a thought experiment about how one can choose to engage in thinking about the monotony one faces in driving in traffic after work and needing to go grocery shopping after a long working day. It is a matter of urgency how one chooses to think about the challenges of navigating the thoughtlessness of other drivers and the inconveniences of putting up with the rude behavior of others at the grocery. By choosing to think otherwise, one might entertain the idea that the person working at the register "is overworked at a job whose daily tedium and meaninglessness surpasses the imagination" and that the car that just cut you off in traffic may be "driven by a father whose little child is hurt or sick in the seat next to him, and he's trying to rush to the hospital."[21]

Instead of responding to the world as it comes at us in the self-centered manner of our default setting, we can decide to interpret the world and behavior of others charitably. As Foster Wallace claims,

> If you're aware enough to give yourself a choice, you can choose to look differently at this fat, dead-eyed, over-made-up lady who just screamed at her kid in the checkout line—maybe she's not usually like this; maybe she's been up three straight nights holding the hand of her husband, who's dying of bone cancer, or maybe this very lady is the low-wage clerk at the motor vehicles department who just yesterday helped your spouse resolve a nightmarish red-tape problem through some small act of bureaucratic kindness.[22]

Foster Wallace contends that those who have really learned to think will know they have alternatives on how to interpret the petty, nerve-wracking experiences of daily life.

This is the real meaning of freedom, tested by the contingencies of daily life: "You get to decide what to worship." In this explicit reference to religion, Foster Wallace remarks that worshipping is a given in human life; it is only a matter of what you choose to worship. Atheism functionally does not exist. This is the reason to worship according to one of the great traditions, because "anything else you worship will eat you alive."[23] One will never have enough if one chooses to worship material things and money. Foster Wallace continues,

> Worship your own body and beauty and sexual allure and you will always feel ugly, and when time and age start showing, you will die a million deaths before they finally plant you.[24]

> Worship power—you will feel weak and afraid, and you will need ever more power over others to keep the fear at bay.[25]

> Worship your intellect, being seen as smart—you will end up feeling stupid, a fraud, always on the verge of being found out.[26]

These forms of worship are "insidious" because they are deeply embedded in each of us as our default setting—how we think, speak, and act without even knowing what we are doing.

Such worship has resulted in a society that is rich in wealth and personal freedom but at the cost of our becoming "lords of our tiny skull-sized kingdoms, alone at the center of all creation."[27] In contrast to this conventional freedom, however, Foster Wallace concludes,

> The really important kind of freedom involves attention, and awareness, and discipline, and effort, and being able truly to care about other people and to sacrifice for them, over and over, in myriad petty little unsexy ways, every day. That is real freedom.[28]

It is unimaginably hard to do this—to live consciously, adultly, day in and day out.[29] This is the truth, according to Foster Wallace, about the meaning of life as spoken to these new college graduates with implications for how we think about Christian freedom in relation to American freedom.

This reflection on the human condition is significant for three reasons related to a Lutheran understanding of Christian freedom. First, the brilliant analysis by Foster Wallace of the human default setting provides a nonreligious interpretation of the theological doctrine of sin, specifically original sin. His conclusions about how the human person is by nature captivated by a default setting of solipsistic self-preoccupation correspond remarkably to the theological tradition's claim

> that we are captive to sin and cannot free ourselves. We have sinned against you [God] in thought, word, and deed, by what we have done and by what we have left undone. We have not loved you with our whole heart; we have not loved our neighbors as ourselves.[30]

While Foster Wallace does not trace the cause of the human condition to alienation from God, his description de facto corresponds to Christian teaching about the nature of sin. His commencement speech is an incredible unveiling of the core human problem expressed in entirely secular terms.

Second, Foster Wallace commends neighbor love as the alternative to remaining thoughtlessly confined to one's default setting. The only way to transcend one's own captivity to egocentricity is to imagine with charity the possible circumstances under which other people may be suffering. In the words of Luther's explanation of the eighth commandment,

> We are to fear and love God, so that we do not tell lies about our neighbors, betray or slander them, or destroy their reputations. Instead we are to come to their defense, speak well of them, and interpret everything they do in the best possible light.[31]

In one sense, Foster Wallace is even more radical than Luther's explanation because Wallace critiques not only how we are to speak about others but even how we *think* about them: "interpret everything they do in the best possible light." This conforms to the teaching of the Great Commandment: "You shall love your neighbor as yourself" (Matt 22:39). Foster Wallace endorses the way of neighborliness as the life-giving alternative to our default setting.

Third—and on this point, the argument of Foster Wallace diverges from the Christian understanding of freedom—the author assumes that human beings have the capacity to fulfill his advice on how to think otherwise about the people one encounters in daily life. He holds that it is within human possibility to maintain a state of consciousness that lends others the benefit of the doubt in how we think about the circumstances of their lives. Here is the divergence from Christian ethics and a Lutheran understanding of human freedom. The possibility of maintaining the altruism Foster Wallace advocates is complicated by the same default setting he so precisely analyzes. Romans 7:15, 19 says, "I do not understand my own actions. For I do not do what I want, but I do the very thing I hate. . . . For I do not do the good I want, but the evil I do not want is what I do." This human limitation prepares us for exploring how it is the gospel of Jesus Christ that prepares the way for living out the ethical life in Christian freedom.

The Freedom of the Gospel in Jesus Christ

The source and origin of Christian freedom, in contrast to American meanings of freedom, is solely the gospel of Jesus Christ. Freedom in Christian theology is totally distinct from those American meanings that refer to lifestyle choices or political, economic, and military facets of freedom. This is the reason confusion abounds when the word *freedom* is employed in the church. Christian freedom derives entirely from the work of Jesus Christ. The gospel of Jesus means free-dom.[32] On the one side, the gospel, as God's good news in Christ Jesus, liberates us from everything that keeps us from being the persons God intended us to be. On the other side, this gospel is the fulcrum within Christian theology that tips toward ethics without itself having ethical content!

Not only does Christian freedom need to be distinguished from the American meanings of freedom explored in this chapter; it is also marked by its unique relationship to the gospel. The gospel of Jesus Christ is unlike any other theological reality; it is sui generis. The gospel is that Word mediated to us by the means of grace, proclamation, and sacraments that has the effect of setting human beings free. Because of this unique location within Christian theology, the character of the gospel commonly gets misunderstood, misappropriated, and misused as a Word that communicates what we are to do as Christians. The gospel itself then becomes a message about ethical expectations and responsibilities, thereby negating its gospel character. While there is an intrinsic relationship between the gospel, Christian freedom, and ethics, it is imperative that we not confuse the gospel with ethics. In classical Lutheran categories, this means we are to distinguish properly between law and gospel.[33]

The law has two classic uses in Lutheran theology.[34] The first, or political, use of the law functions to provide order in society. This includes codes of civil and criminal law by which governments seek to protect communities from harm and curtail wrongdoing. The second—spiritual or theological—use of the law functions to disclose to human beings their fallibility and violations of God's standards and therefore their need for the gospel. This spiritual use of the law convicts us of our sinfulness in order to make us ready to hear and trust the gospel message of forgiveness, grace, and mercy. The gospel is communicated through the spoken word, including preaching, and through the sacraments of baptism and the Lord's Supper. The sacraments are sometimes referred to as "visible words" (Augustine) that deliver the gospel through material signs (water, bread, and wine). The Holy Spirit comes alive through word and sacraments to make the gospel happen.

The gospel has a performative character.[35] It becomes manifest in its very occurrence. This means that the gospel occurs in the very act of its being spoken to us or being administered upon us as sacraments. As the judge in court has the authority to enact the conditions of the law, so the speaker of the gospel or minister of the sacraments has the authority to make the gospel take place. One of the purest forms of gospel expression involves first-person speech: "In the name of Jesus Christ, I declare your sins are forgiven." When such a word is spoken, it is by the efficacious power of this gospel Word that those sins are effectively forgiven in the speaking.

Those who steward the gospel as ministers of word and sacrament are responsible for examining their words carefully to place them in the service of the gospel and to recognize when their words are instead communicating law, either in its first or second use. One of the greatest challenges facing preachers involves thinking you are mediating the gospel when in fact people are hearing law. This occurs most blatantly in religious moralizing about what God wants from us. However, it occurs even more insidiously when the words and teachings of Jesus are cited in the form of a call for our action or under the expectation of our response. Preaching the law when you think you are proclaiming the gospel leaves people dead in their tracks and bereft of the good news.

There are multiple metaphors and images through which the gospel is communicated in Scripture and by which we may share the good news with others. These include not only forgiveness as a central metaphor but reconciliation, salvation, life, gift, grace, mercy, chosen, sacrifice, love, deliverance, liberation, blessed, and resurrection.[36] There is no single way to convey the gospel; rather, the different metaphors and images are like the facets of a diamond, which address the needs of people for hearing the good news in their particular life circumstances and contexts. In every case, when the metaphors or images function as gospel, the recipient receives an unconditional promise and gift from God in Christ. The gospel does not impose demands but lifts burdens and sets one free. The gospel creates a new moment of life. Second Corinthians 5:17 reads, "So if anyone is in Christ, there is a new creation: everything old has passed away; see, everything has become new." The speaking of the gospel is like the original word spoken by God at creation. Thereby something new comes into existence; the gospel creates us anew for Christ's sake.

While the gospel itself is not a message about ethical responsibility, it is the fulcrum (or pivot) in Lutheran theology toward ethics. Mediated by the proclamation of the Word and the administration of the sacraments and by the power of the Holy Spirit, the gospel activates Christian freedom. This Christian freedom is of an entirely different character from the conventional meanings of American freedom or that expressed by Foster Wallace. According to Luther, Christian freedom has two movements, the first in relation to our bondage to sin and the second in relation to the needs of the neighbor. In the classic formulation from his 1520 treatise *The Freedom of a Christian*, Luther explicates the following two theses:

> The Christian individual is a completely free lord of all, subject to none.
> The Christian individual is a completely dutiful servant of all, subject to all.[37]

In effect, the first movement sets the believer free from sin, death, and the power of the devil as Luther names them in *The Small Catechism*. That is, the gospel sets one free from every power that prevents us from being what God intended us to be. In the second movement—and this is emphatic in Lutheran theology—the gospel sets one free for serving neighbors. This emphatic focus on the freedom to serve the neighbor makes Lutheran theology distinctive from many other Protestant formulations whose focus turns on living out one's own righteousness instead of laser focus on living out civil righteousness on behalf of others.

Luther employs an analogy from marriage to describe the means by which this freedom is accomplished:

> Let us examine these things in detail to see how invaluable they are, Christ is full of grace, life, and salvation; the soul is full of sins, death, and damnation. Now let faith intervene and it will turn out that sins, death, and hell are Christ's, but grace, life, and salvation are the soul's. For if he is the groom, then he should simultaneously both accept the things belonging to the bride and impart to the bride those things that are his. For the one who gives his body and his very self to her, how does he not give his all? And the one who receives the body of the bride, how does he not take all that is hers.[38]

With this metaphor, Luther declares the efficacy of the gospel by which the gifts of Christ are imparted to the believer and by which Christian freedom becomes enacted.[39] The gospel works freedom *from* "sins, death, and hell."

Moreover, according to Luther, the gospel works freedom *for* service to neighbors:

> Nevertheless, no one needs even one of these works to attain righteousness and salvation. For this reason, in all of one's works a person should in this

context be shaped by and contemplate this thought alone: to serve and benefit others in everything that may be done; having nothing else in view except the need and advantage of the neighbor.[40]

Whereas other theological programs focus on the righteousness or sanctification of the person saved by God in Christ, Lutheran ethics eschews this turn toward the self and insists that Christian freedom be directed entirely to serving the needs of the neighbor. Given the reality of ecological degradation in our time, we need to expand the horizon of neighbor care to include as neighbors all of creation—earth, waters, and sky, with all their creatures.[41]

There is a fundamental distinction here between the logic of Lutheran ethics and all expressions of Christian theology where primary attention shifts to personal holiness or sanctification of the Christian person.[42] The work of the Holy Spirit in Lutheran theology is mediated by the gospel through the means of grace by which the Christian person is set free to serve neighbors. By contrast, in many holiness traditions, the Holy Spirit is most recognizable in bestowing fruits of the Spirit and gifts of the Spirit that are notable in personal transformation. In accordance with Paul, Lutheran theology sees every gift of the Spirit as a contribution to the "common good" (1 Cor 12:4–7), not as a measure of personal holiness. At Corinth, in fact, appeals to gifts of the Spirit given to a special circle within the congregation are the cause for division (see 1 Cor 3). While there are instances in Lutheran church history where attention has been given to personal holiness, especially within pietistic movements, classical Lutheran Pietism also preserved the momentum of Lutheran theology toward neighbor love through the establishment of educational and diaconal institutions founded to care for those in need, especially those at society's margins.

This chapter has articulated the clear differences between conventional American understandings of freedom and the two aspects of Christian freedom rooted in Lutheran theology. When the term *freedom* refers in everyday discourse to lifestyle, political, economic, and military dimensions of American experience, those seeking to interpret Christian freedom need to be intentional and clear in contrasting these with the Christian meaning through deliberate explanation and definition. Christian freedom has its origin in the gospel of Jesus Christ and comes to expression as freedom from that which holds us in bondage and freedom for serving the neighbor.[43]

Freedom, which in American parlance is about personal and civil rights belonging to citizens, becomes a Christian term that leads us away from preserving our own privileges and toward giving ourselves away in acts of generosity for the sake of others. Even David Foster Wallace, who so insightfully analyzed the trap of self-preoccupation inherent in American notions of freedom, was not able to recognize that the energy source for interpreting the world differently comes from beyond ourselves by the mercy of God.[44] Having given definition to the centrality of the gospel as the source of Christian freedom, we proceed in chapter 4 to locate these central convictions within the larger context of Luther's two kingdoms teaching.

4 Luther's Two Kingdoms as God's Two Strategies

HISTORY HAS BEEN TRAGICALLY MARRED BY the failure of the church of Jesus Christ to actively oppose political tyranny. In the Lutheran tradition, the most ambiguous construct contributing to this failure of political nerve has been the two kingdoms teaching of Martin Luther.[1] The failure of the German Lutheran churches adequately to resist the Nazi regime and the quietism of the Lutheran church in the US regarding political questions are but two examples of the apparent insufficiency of Luther's two kingdoms teaching. Moreover, questions can be raised about the adequacy of this political ethic for Luther himself, especially considering his stance during the rebellion of the peasants and his writings against the Anabaptists and the Jews.[2] Is it possible to reappropriate Luther's two kingdoms teaching as a viable political ethic for the church in its ministry and mission at the beginning of the twenty-first century?

As a poignant instance, the ethics book by Reinhold Seeberg, an influential professor of Dietrich Bonhoeffer, was published posthumously in 1936.[3] Seeberg died in October 1935, after a distinguished career as professor of systematic theology at the University of Berlin. His grandfatherly countenance graces a frontispiece of the book. Taking his framework from Luther, Seeberg presents arguments and arrives at conclusions that in retrospect appear unimaginable: (1) Seeberg minimized the differences between the Confessing Church and the German Christians; (2) with regard to the "Jewish Question," he argued for the impossibility of integrating the Jews into the German Volk; and (3) he defended the moral right of the state to employ eugenics, lest the people and welfare system become overburdened with dependent elderly and handicapped people.[4] How could a Christian ethic based on Luther and Reformation theology arrive at such conclusions?

Misinterpreting the Two Kingdoms

Walter Altmann has sketched four models for church-state relations that distort the relationship of church and state.[5] First, there can be separation of church and state with a demonization of politics. This occurs especially in theologies that focus on salvation as an escape from this evil world. Second, there can be separation of church and state whereby politics is understood to be autonomous from religious influence. This approach functions with a very positive appropriation of the political order as the very instrument of God's creative and ordering power. Altmann cites not only Nazi Germany but also the prevailing interpretation of the separation of church and state in the US as examples of this model. In both instances, religious faith becomes spiritualized and privatized. Third, there can be an alliance of church and state in which the church dominates the state. Medieval Catholicism operated according to this model, as did Calvin's Reformed Church in Geneva. Finally, there can be an alliance of church and state whereby the state dominates the church. Colonial Christianity in Latin America is a specific example and Constantinian Christendom (Caesaropapism) a general example. Altmann offers Luther's two kingdoms teaching as an alternative and more complex model, providing it is interpreted correctly. This has rarely been the case.

Lutherans struggle to understand the significance of Luther's two kingdoms teaching in relationship to Christian responsibility for the sake of the world.[6] This teaching only became a major theological theme in Luther studies in the late nineteenth and early twentieth centuries.[7] Whether two kingdoms was articulated by confessional theologians with a focus on political authority as an "order of creation" or by liberal theologians with a focus on the autonomy of political institutions within the natural order, the consequence was the same: the subservience of the church to the established political order.[8] Increasingly, the nineteenth-century dualism between an autonomous public order and privatized religious devotion was superimposed upon Luther's two kingdoms categories.[9] It was only in the crucible of the use of Luther's two kingdoms teaching by theologians defending National Socialism that the elements of Luther's thought coalesced into the technical designation "*doctrine* of the two kingdoms."[10] Because of the consequences of employing this "doctrine" as an ideological justification for acquiescence of the church to the Nazi movement, it has been severely criticized for leading the church into political quietism.[11] One contemporary commentator argues forcefully that Luther's thinking must be radically reinterpreted if it is to be rendered serviceable in the cause of justice.[12]

In the US, one of the most insidious misunderstandings of Luther's thought involves identifying the two kingdoms wrongly with a misconstrued notion of separation of church and state.[13] Whereas separation of church and state was designed to guarantee that the state impose no mandatory religion upon its citizens, it has been misunderstood to mean that the church should have nothing to do with political debate.[14] According to this view, the two kingdoms should remain two separate realms of activity, with the church relegated to "spiritual" matters while the state is responsible for all things political.[15] One of the most troubling challenges for those committed to the church's political responsibility and engagement in social ministry is the prevailing notion among many church members that the church should stay out of politics. In this misrepresentation, separation of church and state means the church should stick to religious matters as its exclusive task. Pastors in the US regularly face the charge that any advocacy by the church regarding legislation or political policy is out of bounds. The conceptualization of Luther's thought according to two "kingdoms" lends itself very easily to this distortion.

One Kingdom, Two Strategies

Given the host of problems obstructing a constructive interpretation, how might we retrieve the significance of Luther's two kingdoms as an ethical framework advocating the political responsibility of the church? It is crucial to begin with the clear assertion that *finally there is only one kingdom of God.* In his teachings, Jesus spoke extensively about the dawning of God's kingdom. In doing so, Jesus appealed to kingdom as a Jewish metaphor deeply grounded in the Hebrew Bible, as evidenced in the Psalms.[16] The kingdom of God broke into the world in Jesus's sayings, parables, miracles of healing, and casting out demons.[17] The kingdom became present when Jesus forgave sins. The kingdom was present in Jesus's eating with tax collectors and sinners. At his last supper, Jesus instituted a meal of the kingdom for his disciples to share as often as they ate the bread and drank from the cup (Luke 22:14–20). With this meal, Jesus anticipated the eschatological fulfillment of God's kingdom. According to Paul, the kingdom is the destiny of the whole creation (1 Cor 15:24–25).

While the Reformed tradition normally claims there is only one kingdom of God, the Lutheran view entertains complexity about the interaction of church and state according to two "kingdoms" that is muted in Reformed theology. Reformed theology, as represented by American evangelicalism, seeks conformity to the one kingdom of God as its end in both political and ecclesial matters. This approach can blur the means of engagement appropriate to these distinct arenas, leading to efforts to legislate theological positions as public policy.

By contrast, the Lutheran approach is dialectical, encouraging the exercise of political reasoning and inviting coalition building with people of other faiths or no faith at all. Lutheran engagement differentiates between the types of argumentation that are useful when one is operating within the church from a publicly accessible discourse when one engages with those outside the church in the realm of politics. While it would be constructive for Lutheran theology to acknowledge the confusion caused by speaking of "two" kingdoms by appropriating the wisdom of the Reformed tradition in talking about a single kingdom of God, it would be constructive for the Reformed tradition to incorporate the complexity of the Lutheran construct by appropriating the essence of what here is described as two "strategies."

If there are two kingdoms in the New Testament, they are not the kingdoms of church and state. They are instead the kingdoms of God and Satan.[18] In his ministry, Jesus is portrayed as engaging in a cosmic battle, appealing to the power of God versus the rule of Satan (Mark 1:12–13; 1:32–34; 3:22–27; 5:1–13). This is consistent with the cosmic battle between God and the "principalities" and "powers" in the Pauline corpus (cf. Eph 6:12 NKJV). If we are to reappropriate Luther's two kingdoms teaching for theological ethics and the social ministry of the church in our time, we must begin with this fundamental polarity between God and Satan as the framework that also underlies Luther's own thought.[19] An understanding of the cosmic battle between God and Satan is prerequisite for the proper interpretation of what Luther meant by the two kingdoms.

According to Luther's worldview, God employs the angelic powers that inhabit the universe in this battle, while Satan calls upon demonic forces, the principalities and powers. The kingdom of God in this contest would usher forth in a community of justice, truth, hope, love, and freedom, while the kingdom of Satan would bring forth injustice, lies, despair, exploitation, and oppression. In short, the kingdom of God is the kingdom of life, while the kingdom of Satan is one of death. The destiny of the world hangs in the balance as God seeks to subdue Satan's influence over creation. The eschatological hope of Christians, based on the reality of Christ's resurrection, is that ultimately God's kingdom will prevail. In the meantime, however, the outcome remains unclear, as we witness much empirical evidence that Satan has the upper hand.[20]

Given this fundamental contest between God's kingdom and Satan's kingdom in Luther's conceptuality, attempting to distinguish between church and state as two additional "kingdoms" adds complications that generally lead to confusion and misunderstanding. For this reason, some authors have endeavored to speak of two "regiments" or "realms." Unfortunately, such efforts have only contributed another layer of misunderstanding to the entire discussion.[21]

Furthermore, with Luther's two kingdoms teaching, the metaphor of kingdom does not adequately convey the substance of Luther's thought. Kingdom as a *spatial metaphor* leads one to imagine two distinct and separated physical locations that lead to inherent misunderstanding.[22] Luther's two kingdoms teaching is not about two separate and unrelated *realms* but rather about two different types of *divine activity*. The one God—who is the bringer of the one kingdom—engages in two types of activity to oppose the kingdom of Satan. For this reason, I have found it exceedingly effective when interpreting Luther's two kingdoms teaching to refer not to two kingdoms but to *two strategies*.[23] In the contest with the kingdom of Satan, God employs two distinct strategies to thwart Satan's influence and bring forth the one kingdom of God.

The Right- and Left-Hand Strategies

God uses two hands in the battle against Satan: (1) a right-hand strategy that involves the proclamation of the gospel of Jesus Christ and the administration of the holy sacraments of baptism and the Lord's Supper and (2) a left-hand strategy that involves the establishment of just order in society through the institutions of the state, economy, law, education, family, and church.[24] Always these two strategies complement one another; they are never in competition with each other. God is ambidextrous and coordinated in the use of both hands to save and preserve the world. Both strategies serve God's purpose in establishing the one kingdom of God in the world. God is not divided against Godself, pitting one divine kingdom against another. Rather, God employs two strategies to defeat the cause of Satan and usher in the kingdom when God will be all in all.

Both strategies have vital implications for the church's ethical responsibility as expressed in its social ministry. According to *God's right-hand strategy*, sinners are convicted by the law (in its theological use) and condemned as sinners who are in need of redemption. The law in its theological use drives sinners to repentance and convicts them of their need for Christ. The gospel is proclaimed to these convicted sinners as the good news that their sins have been forgiven by the power of the death and resurrection of Jesus Christ. The work of Jesus Christ in word and sacrament is to forgive our sins, deliver us from Satan's power, and bring us to everlasting salvation. The Holy Spirit is alive through the gospel as it comes to us through the means of grace. As we saw in the previous chapter, the Holy Spirit is the power of God to set Christians free—free from sin, death, and the devil—and free for the love of one's neighbor. The *ethical import* of God's right-hand strategy is that Christ sets the sinner *free from* preoccupation with the self and one's own need for salvation and *free for* doing good works solely for the sake of others.[25] The gospel sets Christians free to use their spiritual gifts in service of the neighbor and even to choose suffering on behalf of neighbors in need, including a suffering creation. Herein we discover the ethical significance of Luther's theology of the cross.[26] The gospel frees Christians to take up the cross on behalf of the suffering neighbor, risking solidarity by taking suffering upon themselves for the sake of the neighbor (see chapter 7). The freedom of the gospel is *the* central theological concept for articulating the significance of the Lutheran tradition for ethics.

According to *God's left-hand strategy*, it is God's purpose to provide just structures in society that promote life in the face of Satan's attempts to distort and manipulate them in the service of death. In this strategy, God also employs the law, this time not in its theological use of convicting sinners but rather in its *political use* for ordering the world justly.[27] Although others may not recognize God as a key factor, Christians see God's hand at work wherever fair and equitable civil or criminal statutes are enacted and enforced. Christians are freed by the gospel for genuine concern for the neighbors' welfare. When operating according to this left-hand strategy, they formulate and negotiate arguments to persuade non-Christians to enact laws, policies, or courses of action that promote the welfare of neighbors. Their appeals to publicly accessible reason and enlightened self-interest aim to be persuasive apart from extraordinary pleading based on God's revelation.

While Christians remain centered in their faith in Jesus Christ, they employ common sense and reasoned arguments when operating according to God's left-hand strategy. The primary focus of the left-hand strategy is to approximate the common good for all people and for creation itself, not to promote the self-interest of Christians. For Christians, addressing the well-being of "all" people means drawing special attention to the needs of those most vulnerable to harm and to advocate that civil society address equity in response to their needs for sustainable income, employment opportunities, livable wages, access to medical care, affordable housing, clean water, adequate nutrition, sound public education, and a peaceable life. Provision for the basic necessities of human life needs to have priority in the church's advocacy efforts, defending these as fundamental human rights.

A Lutheran approach to public engagement joins in coalition building with all those who share this commitment to the common good, privileging the needs of the least, whether they are Christian, from other faith traditions, or of no religious affiliation. The focus of Lutheran ethics is on care for the neighbor, whether or not we share the same theological understandings. This distinguishes Lutheran ethics as a commitment to neighbor politics, in contrast to those traditions that insist on religious agreement as a precondition for public engagement. Lutherans can work together for the coming of the Beloved Community with all those of goodwill who are committed to the same goals and strategies to attain them.

God's left-hand strategy places Christians in a variety of life *stations*—as members of a family (child, parent, sibling, spouse, etc.), those engaged in particular kinds of work, members of the church as a public institution, and citizens.[28] In each of these stations, Christians are called to responsibility as they live out their central vocation as baptized persons (see chapter 6). Furthermore, Christians are called to responsibility in the shaping of *institutions themselves* (political, economic, legal, military, educational, religious, etc.) that are just and equitable. Being effective in the enterprise of institution building requires more than winning personal influence over those working or serving within those institutions. The involvement by Christians in advocacy urgently requires concerted effort to exert political power to transform the very structure of public institutions.[29] This includes vigilance about the very shape of those structures that order public life to dismantle structural injustice.

It is not only Christians who are engaged in God's left-hand strategy of living responsibly to advocate for constructing just institutions. All those who live out their life stations with responsibility are employed by God to order and preserve the world against the corrosive and destructive powers of Satan, even when they do not realize they are doing so.[30] Whereas God's right-hand strategy gives explicit reference to God, Christ, and the gospel, in God's left-hand strategy, there are many who would not acknowledge that it is finally God who is sustaining the world through what Luther called "temporal governance."

Christian Political Responsibility

The foundation for Christian political responsibility can be clearly established through this reinterpretation of Luther's two kingdoms teaching. By making explicit how God employs *two distinct strategies* in God's mission of establishing the *one kingdom of God*, we have constructed a framework that avoids the prevalent dangers and misunderstandings that have plagued modern interpreters of Luther's thought.

Other core elements of Luther's theology are preserved in this reinterpretation—above all, law and gospel. Both uses of the law—civil and theological (spiritual) use—have their proper location within the scope of God's work through the two strategies.[31] The first, or civil, use of the law belongs to God's left-hand strategy for guaranteeing just order in society through a rule of law. The second, or theological (spiritual), use of the law belongs to God's right-hand strategy of convicting sinners of their sinfulness and preparing them to hear the gospel of Jesus Christ.

The gospel of Jesus Christ declares the forgiveness of the sinner, who is set free *from* bondage to sin and *for* genuine ethical engagement on behalf of the welfare of neighbors, at the heart of the right-hand strategy. Christian freedom liberates the forgiven sinner for service through both the left- and right-hand strategies—on the left hand through, among other activities, political engagement and on the right hand through evangelizing.[32] The baptismal vocation of the Christian is to be lived out via the several stations afforded to each by God: through relationships with members of the family, at work, as a member of a public church, and in fulfilling the duties of citizenship.

The doctrine of justification by grace through faith in Christ alone, central to the Lutheran tradition, is preserved as the central focus for a proper understanding of what generates the energy leading to Christian political responsibility.[33] Justification by grace through faith in Jesus Christ gives the believer the core identity out of which flow both the left- and right-hand strategies (see chapter 5). By the proclamation of Christ's justifying event on the cross and by his resurrection from the dead, believers come to faith in Christ by the power of the Holy Spirit. Through the saving work of the gospel, Christians are set free *from* their sins, including the primal sin of self-absorption, and are set free *for* paying attention to the needs of their neighbor. Concern for the neighbor takes the form both of left-handed political engagement and of right-handed evangelical outreach. Political advocacy is one indispensable expression of the basic obligation to take seriously the needs of my neighbor by working for societal structures that best approximate and thereby safeguard the basic needs of the neighbor (see chapter 8).

Reclaiming the connection between justification by grace through faith and Christian political responsibility is one of the most urgent theological tasks belonging to Lutheran ethics. Reinterpreting Luther's two kingdoms teaching as God's work of bringing forth the *one kingdom of God through two distinct but complementary strategies* reconnects what tragically became separated in Lutheran church history. In the Lutheran tradition, political quietism has led to disastrous consequences. We must confess our sins and repent, recognizing the inextricable connection between the freedom of the gospel and engagement in political advocacy. God employs two strategies for ruling the world and inaugurating the kingdom of *shalom*.[34] Christians serve God by living responsibly not only by testifying to the gospel of Jesus Christ but at the same time by their active political engagement.

5 Justification and Sanctification

ONE OF THE MOST CHALLENGING PROBLEMS for Lutheran theology and ethics involves the relationship between the doctrine of justification and the activation of the Christian life, specifically the understanding of sanctification. Martin Luther himself operated with a robust understanding of the active involvement of the Holy Spirit in the life of the church, particularly as mediated through word and sacraments.[1] Through the Word of God—Jesus Christ, Scripture, and proclamation as the three central expressions—and through the sacraments of Holy Baptism and the Lord's Supper as means of grace, the Holy Spirit mediates the gifts of Jesus Christ. Luther writes in *The Small Catechism*,

> I believe that by my own understanding or strength I cannot believe in Jesus Christ my LORD or come to him, but instead the Holy Spirit has called me through the gospel, enlightened me with his gifts, made me holy and kept me in the true faith, just as he calls, gathers, enlightens, and makes holy the whole Christian church on earth and keeps it with Jesus Christ in the one common, true faith. Daily in this Christian church the Holy Spirit abundantly forgives all sins—mine and those of all believers. On the Last Day the Holy Spirit will raise me and all the dead and will give me and all believers in Christ eternal life. This is most certainly true.[2]

The Holy Spirit works through the gospel to bestow spiritual gifts on the whole church. Lutheran theology centers itself on the gospel of Jesus Christ (see chapter 3). While the Holy Spirit can and does work in other ways, the Lutheran focus is on the Spirit working through the means of grace—word and sacraments—where Jesus Christ has promised to reveal himself. Through these means of grace, Jesus Christ brings all promised gifts: forgiveness of sin, deliverance from death and the power of the devil, and eternal life.[3]

The Centrality of the Doctrine of Justification

Lutheran ethics interweaves the work of the Holy Spirit inextricably with the work of Jesus Christ in relation to the Christian life. Due to the theological controversies that gave rise to the Reformation, the central matter was justification by grace alone through faith alone in Christ alone, not sanctification. The insistence on "alone" (*sola*) highlights what was at stake in the theological dispute at that time: whether good works performed by human beings are necessary for salvation. Many of the pious practices of the late-medieval period obscured the gospel of Jesus Christ as the exclusive basis for divine salvation. Pious works were understood to earn merit before God through the performance of private masses, making pilgrimages, reverencing relics, or purchasing indulgences. Such acts of human piety performed to earn salvation were criticized by Lutherans as works righteousness. Salvation is based on the alien righteousness that is received by the work of Jesus Christ, not based on any righteousness performed by human beings. Justification is based on the passive righteousness of faith received as gift by trusting in Jesus Christ alone. The primary focus in the Lutheran tradition is on the holiness of Jesus Christ that is ascribed to the believer by faith in Christ's justifying work, not on a holiness attained through the Christian life.

In the Augsburg Confession, justification was confessed as the central article of faith:

> Likewise, they teach that human beings cannot be justified before God by their own powers, merits, or works. But they are justified as a gift on account of Christ's sake through faith when we believe that Christ has suffered for us and that for his sake our sin is forgiven and righteousness and eternal life are given to us. For God will regard and reckon this faith as righteousness in his sight, as St. Paul says in Romans 3[:21–26] and 4[:5].[4]

Luther wrote about justification in *The Smalcald Articles*, one of the Lutheran Confessional writings, asserting, "Nothing in this article can be conceded or given up, even if heaven and earth or whatever is transitory passed away."[5]

Lutheran theology centers itself on the doctrine of justification as the article by which the church stands or falls according to Scripture, the Lutheran Confessions, and Lutheran doctrine. Furthermore, justification by grace through faith in Jesus Christ remains the central article of teaching for every generation.[6]

The laser focus on justification within the theological controversies of the Reformation created a theological dilemma for all subsequent efforts by Lutherans to interpret the Christian life. The relationship between justification and sanctification remains an unresolved challenge for Lutheran ethics. This dilemma is illustrated by the claim of Gerhard Forde that "sanctification, if it is to be spoken of as something other than justification, is perhaps best defined as the art of getting used to the unconditional justification wrought by the grace of God for Jesus' sake."[7] Such a claim reduces sanctification to an extension in time of living by justification alone.

The most trenchant and enduring critique of Lutheran theology's limitations in failing to address the implications of justification for the Christian life is by Dietrich Bonhoeffer in his book *Discipleship*. This analysis is all the more significant insofar as it was issued by a theologian who organized his entire theology out of the christological center derived from the doctrine of justification. Bonhoeffer's criticism of "cheap grace" in contrast to "costly grace" remains the most incisive diagnosis of this Lutheran Achilles' heel.

Writing amid the catastrophe of Nazi Germany, Bonhoeffer denounced the failure of Lutheran theology to generate a life of discipleship:

> Like ravens we have gathered around the carcass of cheap grace. From it we have imbibed the poison which has killed the following of Jesus among us. The doctrine of pure grace experienced an unprecedented deification. The pure doctrine of grace became its own God, grace itself. Luther's teachings are quoted everywhere but twisted from their truth into self-delusion. They say if only our church is in possession of a doctrine of justification, then it is surely a justified church! They say Luther's true legacy should be recognizable in making grace as cheap as possible. Being Lutheran should mean that discipleship is left to the legalists, Reformed, or the enthusiasts, all for the sake of grace. They say that the world is justified and Christians in discipleship are made out to be heretics. A people began Christian, became Lutheran, but at the cost of discipleship, at an all-too-cheap price. Cheap grace had won.[8]

Bonhoeffer's critique delivers the point of departure for the remainder of this chapter and the next.

Bonhoeffer offered a remedy by calling for costly grace—based on the actual death and resurrection of the Christian person in conformity to baptism as being joined to the death and resurrection of Jesus Christ—that issues forth in a life of discipleship. *Discipleship* is Bonhoeffer's manual for the Christian life in the form of a commentary on the Sermon on the Mount. Unlike Lutheran theologians before him, Bonhoeffer discovered that the Sermon on the Mount was not merely a set of impossible demands functioning as law to drive the sinner to justification. Instead, Bonhoeffer argued that the Sermon on the Mount provides actual instructions for Christian discipleship. Discipleship becomes the meaning of sanctification in the Lutheran tradition.

The Problem of Relating Justification and Sanctification

Luther's *The Freedom of a Christian* is key for interpreting his understanding of the relationship between justification and the Christian life (see chapter 3). According to Luther, the gospel of Jesus Christ means freedom. He articulates the twofold meaning of Christian freedom according to the following intriguing formula:

> A Christian is a perfectly free lord of all, subject to none.
> A Christian is a perfectly dutiful servant of all, subject to all.[9]

The first thesis pertains to justification. A Christian is not subject to any lords except to Jesus Christ alone. The lordship of Jesus Christ is exercised according to the logic of justification by faith alone. Luther elaborates on the meaning of faith for the Christian life: "Faith alone is the saving and efficacious use of the Word of God." The gifts of Jesus Christ become the gifts of the sinner, who becomes saint through a sweet exchange. Luther writes, "Christ is full of grace, life, and salvation. The soul is full of sins, death, and damnation. Now let faith come between them and sins, death, and damnation will be Christ's, while grace, life, and salvation will be the soul's."[10] By faith, the sinner receives freedom *from* sin, death, and the devil.

The second thesis pertains to service of neighbors. Not only does the gospel of Jesus Christ set sinners free from bondage; the gospel also sets Christians free *for* the service of others. Whereas good works performed to demonstrate one's worthiness before God are precluded by Luther as works righteousness, good works performed in service to others are the proper expression of civic righteousness. While good works do not justify the sinner before God, the proper and necessary performance of good works is always in service to the needs of the neighbor. According to Luther, "Here faith is truly active through love [Gal 5:6], that is, it finds expression in works of the freest service, cheerfully and lovingly done, with which [one] willingly serves another without hope of reward."[11]

The same line of thought is found in Luther's *Two Kinds of Righteousness*. The first form of righteousness is "alien righteousness, that is the righteousness of another, instilled from without. This is the righteousness of Christ by which he justifies through faith." The second form of righteousness is "proper righteousness, not because we alone work it, but because we work with that first and alien righteousness." Proper righteousness involves both the death of the sinful self and the rising up of the new self in Christ. The second form of "righteousness consists in love to one's neighbor."[12] This focus on serving the neighbor comes to expression in Luther's theology through his doctrine of vocation, with baptism as the call to serve others in all stations of daily life.

In contrast to other Christian traditions, there are two kinds of "holiness" for Luther. The first is passive holiness, which is received from Jesus Christ as a gift. The work of Christ gives us his own holiness as a gift through the power of the Holy Spirit mediated through the gospel. This gift is received in gratitude by faith alone. The second is active holiness as the gospel sets us free for good works on behalf of others. This might be described as "social holiness" lived out in service to neighbors.

Philip Melanchthon articulated another category for considering the Christian life: the *third use of the law*, a theme that was subsequently taken up by the Lutheran Confessions. In contrast to the first (or political) use of the law, which governs society, and the second (or theological) use of the law, which discloses human sinfulness by preparing the sinner to receive the gospel, the third use was to function as a guide to the Christian life. Melanchthon wrote in the 1543 edition of *Loci Communes*,

> The third use of the Law pertains to the regenerate. Insofar as the regenerate have been justified by faith, they are free from the Law. . . . Yet in the meantime it must be said that the Law which points out the remnants of

sin, in order that the knowledge of sin and repentance may increase, and the gospel also must proclaim Christ in order that faith may grow. Furthermore, the Law must be preached to the regenerate to teach them certain works in which God wills that we practice obedience.[13]

While there has been extensive debate about the third use of the law, especially for Luther's thought and its standing in Lutheran theology, affirmation of a third use of the law became an early and enduring category for addressing the problem of sanctification in the Lutheran tradition.[14] The third use of the law affirmed that believers continue to need the direction of God's law to practice obedience to God's commands.

The *Formula of Concord*, the last of the confessional writings in the *Book of Concord*, describes the third use of the law as a "guide" for life: "third, after they have been reborn—since nevertheless the flesh still clings to them—that precisely because of the flesh they may have a sure guide, according to which they can orient and conduct their entire life."[15] The article on "Concerning the Third Use of the Law" addressed controversies that had broken out among Lutheran theologians about legalism versus antinomianism and whether the law still applied to Christians and not just to "unbelievers, non-Christians, and the unrepentant".[16]

> Therefore, for both the repentant and unrepentant, for the reborn and those not reborn, the law is and remains one single law, the unchangeable will of God. In terms of obedience to it there is a difference only in that those people who are not yet reborn do what the law demands unwillingly, because they are coerced (as is also the case with the reborn with respect to the flesh). Believers, however, do without coercion, with a willing spirit, insofar as they are born anew, what no threat of the law could ever force from them.[17]

Whereas Luther placed central emphasis on the freedom of the gospel for serving neighbors as an expression of social holiness, here we see an emerging interest in the quality of the Christian life among believers in contrast to those not reborn. This is how Lutheran theology sought to address the nature of sanctification and the Christian life. While Lutheran teaching never eclipsed the primary focus on social holiness, Lutheran theologians increasingly sought to explore the character of personal holiness in relation to sanctification.

With Lutheran Orthodoxy in the seventeenth and eighteenth centuries, we see a return to the organization of theology according to the Aristotelian categories that characterized medieval scholastic theology. The compendium of writings by Lutheran Orthodox theologians compiled by Heinrich Schmid documents the analysis of justification into component elements. Justification is a divine forensic act, embracing (1) the forgiveness of sins and (2) the imputation of the righteousness of Christ but also the "concomitants and consequences of justifying faith."[18] Included among these consequences are (1) vocation, (2) illumination (by the Holy Spirit), (3) regeneration and conversion, (4) mystical union, and (5) renovation.[19]

Quoting the work of David Hollatz (1646–1702) as representative, Schmid summarizes the teaching of the Lutheran Orthodox theologians on *renovation*:

> Renovation is an act of grace, whereby the Holy Spirit, expelling the faults of a justified man, endows him with inherent sanctity. The change that takes place in man consists further in this, that by the influence of divine grace the sin still cleaving to man disappears, more and more, and gives place to an increasing facility for doing what is good. As, however, the sinfulness yet remaining in man yields only through constantly repeated struggle against sin, this renovation is not sudden, but a gradual one, susceptible of constant growth; and as sin never entirely leaves man, it is never perfect, although we are always to strive after perfection. Finally, it is a work of God in man, yet of such a nature that there is a free co-operation on the part of man, who now in conversion has received new spiritual powers.[20]

Three features of Lutheran Orthodox theology are noteworthy in relation to the Christian life: (1) the antecedent of all matters related to sanctification remains God's justification by grace through faith in Christ alone, (2) a resistance to every Christian perfectionism according to the understanding that the one made holy by Christ remains at the same time sinner (*simul justus et peccator*), and (3) renovation remains God's work through the power of the Holy Spirit. It is interesting that Schmid includes a section on "good works" only as a supplement to the extended discussion of the consequences of justifying faith:[21] "Renovation makes itself known by good works . . . not, indeed, as though they had thereby to justify themselves before God, or to merit their salvation (for unless they were justified, they could not perform good works) but because they thereby show their obedience toward God . . ."[22]

Whereas many interpreters have been prone to stress only discontinuity, the discussion of renovation in Lutheran Orthodoxy demonstrates continuity with developments that emerged during the period of Lutheran Pietism. Philipp Jakob Spener (1635–1705) is the author of the classical work *Pia Desideria* (Pious longings), or *Heartfelt Desires for Improvement Pleasing to God of the True Evangelical Churches, including Some Christian Recommendations to That End*, published in 1675.[23] In part 3, Spener sets forth six proposals for reform, the first two drawn from Luther and the latter four from Johann Arndt (1555–1621): (1) Bible reading by families in homes and by individuals, reading books of the Bible at church services, and meetings during the week for "mutual instruction and edification"; (2) establishing "the spiritual priesthood" to all believers for mutual encouragement and admonition; (3) teaching that the Christian faith means practice, not just knowledge; (4) showing love and praying for unbelievers; (5) reforming the education of pastors; and (6) sermons focused more on forming listeners in faith and love, less on theological erudition.[24]

Other major figures of German Pietism included August Hermann Francke (1663–1727) at Halle and Count Nicolaus von Zinzendorf (1700–1760), Moravian bishop at Herrnhut. Douglas H. Shantz summarizes the contributions of German Pietism:

> The genius of Pietism lay in the adjectives it employed: *true* Christianity; *heartfelt, living* faith; a *living* knowledge of God; the *inward* Christ and the *inner* word. Another set of adjectives expressed Pietist hopes for renewal of humanity and a better future for the church: the *new* man, *born-again* Christianity, the coming *Philadelphian* church. Born-again laypeople became agents of their own spirituality, reading the Bible for themselves and teaching and encouraging one another in non-church settings.[25]

Such practices conform to holiness movements in other Christian traditions. For Lutheran theology, however, these emerge under the doctrinal presupposition of justification by faith. Those influenced by Lutheran Pietism carry forward these emphases into the nineteenth and twentieth centuries.

The full communion agreement between the Evangelical Lutheran Church in America and the Moravian Church in America, *Following Our Shepherd to Full*

Communion, provides a fascinating instance of how ecumenical rapprochement can contribute new insights in relation to Lutheran teaching. The section on "Mutual Complementarities" takes up the topic, "The Holy Spirit, the Believer, and the Christian Life." After affirming that both traditions share the core commitment to justification by faith apart from works of law, the agreement offers a complementary understanding from the Moravian tradition:

> The Moravian experience of the Spirit in the life of the believer was not shaped by the polemics of the Reformation but by the Brethren's endurance in the Ancient Church, the "period of the hidden seed," its renewal in Continental Pietism, and its internal struggles to be faithful to the power of the Spirit and the need for witnessing to Christ as individuals and as a community. . . . Moravians and Lutherans complement each other in agreeing on the point of need for the Spirit in engendering faith through our central affirmation of justification through grace by means of the Spirit. Lutherans seek to maintain the grace of God bestowed through the Spirit against any shadow of human works and worth. The Unity endeavors to ensure that the believer realizes justification opens a gracious relationship with Jesus by means of the Spirit.[26]

This is a promising fruit of ecumenical work between two traditions that share common doctrinal roots. By focusing more explicitly on the work of the Spirit as "the source and power of sanctification in the life of the believer," Lutherans might reclaim more fulsomely Luther's own robust understanding of the Spirit in relating sanctification inextricably to justification. The Moravian emphasis on "the continual presence and activity of the Spirit within the believer . . . calling them to live according to their calling to holiness and eternal life" can offer the Lutheran tradition a new perspective.[27]

Contemporary Approaches Relating Justification and Sanctification

Four contributions from recent theology deserve mention concerning the relation of justification to sanctification: ongoing advocacy for third use of the law (Murray), the proposal for a second use of the gospel (Lazareth), insistence on a life of discipleship (Bonhoeffer), and Finnish scholarship on the indwelling

Christ (Mannermaa). Each of these approaches deserves attention as we draw conclusions about resolving this problem.

Scott R. Murray has provided an important survey of the third use of the law in American Lutheranism from 1940 to 2000. His research documents how the third use of the law remains highly contested among American Lutheran theologians. Those who reject third use of the law do so primarily to avoid the reintroduction of a new legalism into Lutheran theology. Those who defend the third use of the law do so to ward off antinomianism in the form of "gospel reductionism": "Supporters of the third use of the Law warned that by denying it the church would fall into moral laxity."[28] According to this view, a third use of the law is necessary to hold in check the sinner self.

Whether Luther himself can be cited as an authority for a third use of the law remains an open question. This leads to ongoing speculation about whether it is a useful constructive category, even though it was affirmed by Melanchthon and the *Formula of Concord*. The centrality of justification by faith in Christ alone can become displaced from the center of Lutheran theology by the dictates of the law according to a third use. Those who are averse to a third use of the law place central focus on the freedom of the gospel as the fulcrum between justification and Lutheran ethics.

William H. Lazareth makes an idiosyncratic proposal by interpreting Luther according to a "second or parenetic use of the gospel." Instead of reverting to the third use of the law to interpret the Christian life, Lazareth affirms a *second use of the gospel* as "faith working through love."[29] He locates the discussion of a second use of the gospel in relation to the locus of natural law and the first use of the law within Lutheran categories:

> It goes without saying that the law's sin-related theological and political functions also apply to imperfect Christians insofar as they still remain sinful. However, insofar as they are already righteous, it is rather the gospel's parenetic or ethical function, under the indwelling Holy Spirit's governance, to empower and guide the joyful fulfillment of God's pre-fall and perennial command of dominion-sharing love by God's renewed Christian workers serving as responsible members of church and society.[30]

The operative theological category undergirding Lazareth's proposal is *simul justus et peccator*—that the Christian remains sinner and saint simultaneously. For

Christians, "the parenetic function of God's gospel interpenetrates the political function of God's law for our vocational sanctification in daily life."[31] This is not so much a matter of personal holiness but instead stresses public holiness for the sake of serving neighbors.

Both the third use of the law and Lazareth's unconventional reference to a second use of the gospel appear to be failed efforts to address the disputed question about how to explain the Christian life. By contrast, the proposals of Dietrich Bonhoeffer and Tuomo Mannermaa are especially significant as constructive contributions about the relationship of justification and sanctification.

Bonhoeffer's *Discipleship* is vital not only for his criticism of cheap grace but also for constructing a thoroughgoing christological interpretation of the Christian life as discipleship. Bonhoeffer is hyper-Lutheran in the christocentric focus of his thought from beginning to end. *Discipleship* is a theological commentary on the Sermon on the Mount that formulates the pattern of the Christian life from the teaching of Jesus. This deviates significantly from traditional Lutheran interpretations of the Sermon as unfulfillable expectations that are designed to convince the sinner of the need for forgiveness (the second or theological use of the law).

Consistent with Luther himself, Bonhoeffer asserts that both justification and sanctification "spring from the same source, namely Jesus Christ, the crucified one."[32] In baptismal terms, the Christian life involves daily death to sin and daily resurrection to Jesus Christ. This means complete dependence on the righteousness that is received as gift by the work of Jesus Christ. Bonhoeffer proceeds, however, to make the following distinction between justification and sanctification:

> Both gifts belong inseparably together. However, just because of this connection between them, they are not simply one and the same. While justification appropriates to Christians the deed God has already accomplished, sanctification promises them God's present and future action. Whereas, in justification, believers are being included in the community with Jesus Christ through Christ's death that took place once and for all; sanctification, on the other hand, preserves them in the sphere into which they have been placed. It keeps them in Christ, within the church-community.[33]

It is imperative to notice how Bonhoeffer shifts the focus in sanctification from the individual to the church community.

Sanctification is Christ's gift to the communion of saints. Both the communal character of sanctification according to God's holiness (which forms the church as a "contrast community"[34]) and the hiddenness of that sanctification are noteworthy. Bonhoeffer writes,

> For the community of saints this implies three things. *First*, its sanctification will manifest itself *in a clear separation from the world*. Its sanctification will, *second*, prove itself through *conduct* that is *worthy* of God's realm of holiness. And, *third*, its sanctification will be *hidden in waiting* for the day of Jesus Christ.[35]

Whatever holiness is demonstrated by the church community is "hidden with Christ in God" (Col 3:3). Neither the individual nor the discipleship community can claim merit (or even knowledge) of their sanctification. Bonhoeffer says, "Sanctification always relates to the end of time. Its goal is not to pass the test when judged by the world or even by the person being sanctified, but to pass the test of the Lord."[36] All belongs to Jesus Christ.

The most innovative rendering of the inextricable relationship between justification and sanctification has been developed by the Finnish school of Luther scholarship, whose seminal figure is Tuomo Mannermaa. What is original in this interpretation of Luther's thought is the shift from a forensic understanding of Christ's justifying work toward the real presence of Jesus Christ dwelling within the believer to accomplish both justification and sanctification. According to Mannermaa,

> In faith, human beings are really united with Christ. Christ, in turn, is both the forgiveness of sins and the effective producer of everything that is good in them. Therefore "sanctification"—that is, the sanctity or holiness of the Christian—is, in fact, only another name for the same phenomenon of which Luther speaks when discussing the communication of attributes, the happy exchange, and the union between the person of Christ and the believer.[37]

This approach provides a breakthrough in the history of Luther interpretation. Mannermaa makes two incisive points regarding holiness: (1) "the holiness of Christians is totally based on 'external signs,' that is, on word and sacraments," and (2) "Christians' holiness is also not based on their ability to avoid heresies in doctrine or life." This leads him to affirm, as did Bonhoeffer, "the hidden holiness of the church."[38]

The Finnish school, following Mannermaa, claims to have resolved this central problem in Luther scholarship:

> Unlike the *Formula of Concord* and later Lutheran theology, Luther does not separate justification and the presence of Christ in the believer. . . . The idea of Christ's real presence in faith sheds light on the meaning of many of those themes in Luther's theology that have continued to be subjects of controversy among scholars up to the present day. This idea makes apprehensible the Reformer's understanding of the relationships between justification and sanctification, real and declarative righteousness, and the partial and total aspects of the idea of "simultaneously righteous and a sinner."[39]

On the strength of this scholarship, it is possible to conclude with two central theological convictions that need to be maintained in understanding the relation of justification to sanctification.

First, Lutheran ethics must be interpreted according to the *centripetal force* of Christology. Justification by grace through faith in Christ alone centers the universe of Lutheran thought. Holiness, like righteousness in its alien form, is a gift to be received passively for Christ's sake. There is no place for Christian perfectionism in Lutheran theology. The Christian always remains under the proviso of being sinner and saint simultaneously (*simul justus et peccator*). This means that sanctification must ultimately be interpreted entirely as the gift of the indwelling Jesus Christ, for which gift the believer can only offer thanks and gratitude. The Christian life is a generous response to the Great Thanksgiving of what God has done for the world in Jesus Christ.

Second, the *centrifugal force* of the gospel of Jesus Christ shifts attention away from personal holiness to social holiness. The gospel of Jesus Christ sets the believer not only free *from* the power of sin, death, and the devil but, even more, free *for* service to the neighbor in daily life. Holiness, like righteousness in its civil form, involves the ethical response of neighborliness to others in the arenas of home, work, local community, citizenship, and globe. Luther's doctrine of vocation is grounded in baptism as a call to serve other people—and creation itself—as neighbors.[40] Baptismal vocation is foundational for Luther's understanding of the universal priesthood of all believers, one of the most original gifts of the Lutheran Reformation.[41] Only the retrieval of Luther's robust understanding of vocation and the universal priesthood can give expression to the social holiness that is the final goal of the Christian life. This central theme is addressed in the next chapter.

6 Vocation of the Universal Priesthood

MARTIN LUTHER'S TEACHING ABOUT THE UNIVERSAL priesthood remains an *unfulfilled promise of the Reformation*. If justification and vocation are the twin pillars of the Lutheran Reformation, the bearers of this legacy over the centuries have secured the prominent place of justification while at the same time relegating vocation to a marginal position, never fulfilling the promise of Luther's teaching about the universal priesthood.[1] Instead of developing the fulsome potential of Luther's theology of vocation in tandem with justification, the universal priesthood of all believers lived out in the arenas of their daily lives has remained sidelined.

Justification belongs to the heart of Luther's Reformation breakthrough as he rediscovered the power of grace in Jesus Christ: "They are now justified by his grace as a gift, through the redemption that is in Christ Jesus" (Rom 3:24). Justification by grace alone through faith alone in Christ alone has been rightly articulated and defended as the article upon which "stands all that we teach and practice."[2] Justification also has been granted a central place in unprecedented ecumenical breakthroughs, especially with the Roman Catholic Church at the signing of the monumental *Joint Declaration on the Doctrine of Justification*.[3]

At the same time, we must declare that the Reformation tradition has failed organically to connect the doctrine of justification with living out the Christian life. Dietrich Bonhoeffer analyzed this deficit in his classic book *Discipleship* when he described the victory of "cheap grace" at the expense of following Jesus Christ (see chapter 5). A single-minded focus on justification prompted an interruption between faith and good works that has been the Achilles' heel of Lutheran theology over the centuries. The solution to this age-old problem, however, depends on retrieving Luther's robust understanding of vocation and giving prominence to the universal priesthood in organic relationship to the doctrine of justification.

Jürgen Moltmann affirms vocation as "the third great insight of the Reformation" after word and sacrament.[4] When Luther deconstructed the "three walls" built to defend the power of the late-medieval Roman Catholic Church—ecclesial claims to superiority over temporal power, ecclesial claims to authority above the interpretation of Scripture, and excessive claims to papal authority—he did so to recover the equal status of all the baptized alongside priests, bishops, and popes: "This is because we all have one baptism, one gospel, one faith, and are all Christians alike; for baptism, gospel, and faith alone make us spiritual and a Christian people."[5]

Luther stressed the extent of this equal status:

> To put it still more clearly: suppose a group of earnest Christian laymen were taken prisoner and set down in a desert without an episcopally ordained priest among them. And suppose they were to come to a common mind there and then in the desert and elect one of their number, whether he were married or not, and charge him to baptize, say mass, pronounce absolution, and preach the gospel. Such a [person] would be as truly a priest as though he had been ordained by all the bishops and popes in the world. That is why in cases of necessity anyone can baptize and give absolution. This would be impossible if we were not all priests.[6]

This is not about diminishing the service of pastors as ministers of word and sacrament. Pastors have a crucial role and calling in a theology of ministry oriented toward the ministry of the baptized. Rather, this is specifically about *the equal status of all Christian persons* by virtue of baptism and baptism alone.[7] The central claim is this: *baptism is the primary ordination of all Christians.* Therefore, the retrieval of a robust understanding of vocation is urgently needed to reform the church in service to neighbors for the life of the world and integrity of creation.

Freedom for Baptismal Vocation in the Arenas of Daily Life

Luther's construction of the universal priesthood began as an attack on elevated status claimed for the offices of priest and bishop. Nathan Montover writes, "In this way, Luther rejected the notion of a twofold priesthood: a spiritual and an external priesthood. For Luther, there exists only one priesthood: the spiritual priesthood."[8] The responsibility of serving as a teacher of the Word belongs to all Christians. While the community designates particular persons to the "external priesthood" for the sake of church order to preach and administer sacraments by a public call, this is not an elevation to a higher, godlier status. Luther writes,

> Thus we all, as I have said before, have become priest's children through baptism. Therefore it should be understood that the name "priest" ought to be the common possession of believers just as much as the name "Christian" or "Child of God."[9]

God grants freedom to all followers of Christ "so that all of us should proclaim God's Word and works at every time and in every place, and persons from all ranks, races, and stations may be specially called to the ministry, if they have the grace and the understanding of Scriptures to teach others."[10]

Montover summarizes Luther's views on the universal priesthood according to the following themes: (1) sometimes it serves as an attack on the authority of the pope (as against the "three walls"); (2) the ministry of the ordained is to be limited so that it remains a service to, not lordship over, all; (3) it is a call "for renewed commitment to Christian life"; and (4) on occasion, it "is used as a tool for understanding—or influencing—the political realm."[11]

As we have seen, the key text for interpreting a proper understanding of the relationship between justification and vocation in Luther's thought is *The Freedom of a Christian*, with its two central affirmations: (1) a Christian is lord of all, completely free of everything, and (2) a Christian is a servant, completely attentive to the needs of all.[12] While the first affirmation articulates the power of the gospel to set the Christian free *from* everything that prevents us from living as the persons God created us to be, it is not complete without the second. Because of Christ's work, Christian persons do not need to worry or be preoccupied about their status or worth in relationship to God. We are the beloved ones of God, whose sins are forgiven. We need no longer be troubled about our inherent worth or dignity in relationship to God.

Exactly because Christ sets us free from all things that sever our relationship with God, now our attention can be redirected from preoccupation with what God thinks about us to focus instead on what our neighbor needs from us (Luther's second affirmation). God, for Christ's sake, does not need our good works; it is our neighbor who does need our good works. Luther says,

> Now we ought to know that we are named after Christ—and not because he is absent but precisely because he dwells in our midst! Our trust in him means that we are Christs to one another and act toward our neighbors as Christ has acted toward us.[13]

This is the proper use of good works—in relationship to the needs of the neighbor and not for pleasing God, who has already been sufficiently pleased by what Christ has accomplished.[14] Luther continues, "This teaching tells us that the good we have from God should flow from one to the other and be common to all. Everyone should 'put on' the neighbor and act toward him or her as if we were in the neighbor's place. The good that flowed from Christ flows into us."[15]

Luther does not leave this teaching about neighbor love abstract, however. If it is the case that *all Christians share a single status (Stand)* in this world by virtue of our singular baptism into Christ, there are distinct arenas in which Christians live out their love of neighbor in the world:[16]

> The first [arena] is that of the home, from which the people come. The second is that of the state, that is, the country, the people, princes, and lords, which we call the temporal [arena]. These two [arenas] embrace everything: children, property, money, animals, and so on. The home must produce, whereas the city must guard, protect, and defend. Then follows the third, God's own home and city, that is, the Church, which must obtain people from the home and protection and defense from the state. These are the three hierarchies ordained by God . . . the three high divine [arenas], the three divine, natural and temporal laws of God.[17]

It is important to add that it is not only Christians who serve others through such distinct arenas of service, but all human beings, whether they recognize or acknowledge it, serve God insofar as they render service to the neighbors they encounter in their daily lives.[18]

In his teaching about the arenas (offices/estates), Luther identifies three primary spheres in which Christians live out their baptismal vocation: (1) marriage/family, (2) government/state, and (3) church.[19] In the sixteenth century, the first arena, marriage/family, encompassed the responsibilities of both the household and economic life. Given the divergence of economic activity beyond the home in subsequent history, it is appropriate now to distinguish four arenas for living out one's vocation: family, work, government, and church (or religious institution, in the case of other faiths).

Service to the neighbor takes place in these specific arenas of daily life where the baptized are located. Wingren affirms,

> With persons as his "hands" or "coworkers," God gives his gifts through the earthly vocations (food through farmers, fishermen and hunters; external peace through princes, judges, and orderly powers; knowledge and education through teachers and parents, etc.).[20]

We serve the neighbors God gives us in our own family, in our workplace or at school, in public life, and through religious institutions (the church). These are the primary arenas where the baptized are called to love and serve other people as neighbors. Kathryn A. Kleinhans writes, "Humans are called to exercise stewardship within these organizing structures, working to preserve the created world. Given the hierarchical nature of society in Luther's time, his insistence that one's callings are located within the same social structures as everyone else was particularly important. All people have genuine callings from God, and those callings are located within, rather than outside of, ordinary human experience."[21] Moreover, it is urgent for us to add that each of these spheres of influence is located within the context of creation, whose elements, flora, and fauna we are also to love as neighbors from God.

The baptized live out their callings by serving neighbors in their arenas of daily life. As Luther says,

> Each shoemaker, smith, farmer and the like has his own office and trade, and nevertheless all are equally consecrated priests and bishops. And each with his office or work ought to provide aid and service to the others, so that all kinds of work can be set up in a community to support body and soul, just as the members of the body all serve each other.[22]

For example, in the family, the baptized serve as ministers to their neighbors as a son/daughter, sister/brother, aunt/uncle, spouse, or parent. In the workplace or in school, the baptized serve neighbors through diligence for the sake of neighbors in their particular responsibilities and relationships in this arena. In the public life, the baptized care for the common good, for example, through volunteer work, caring for creation, or participating in the political process. Globally, the baptized serve neighbors, for example, through mutual relationships of accompaniment, generosity in sharing, and social advocacy.

Churchification of Ministry as the New Babylonian Captivity

The church, at least in North America and Europe, faces a Babylonian captivity as all-encompassing and debilitating as that criticized by Luther in the sixteenth century. At that time, the Babylonian captivity involved the church's usurpation of power over every facet of human life, asserting authority to control each and every arena. Today the Babylonian captivity of the church, although differently guised, is equally deadly for the vitality of the church's mission: the reduction of Christian ministry to that which is done in the name of the institutional church. Church members largely think that only what is organized by the institutional church or done within the confines of a church building really counts as Christian ministry.

Since the time of the Reformation, another mighty wall has been constructed that is aimed at securing the self-interest of the church as institution: the compartmentalization of Christian existence by confining it to those activities organized and conducted by the institutional church. This represents the "churchification" of Christian ministry. While leaders of the institutional church may pay lip service to the universal priesthood of all believers, primary attention at outreach involves securing financial resources and new members for the sake of the survival of the church as institution. The gap between what happens in and for the institutional church, especially on Sundays, and the involvement of people the rest of the week has become enormous.

Whereas in North America and Europe a deep rift exists between what happens in the name of the institutional church and the rest of people's lives, in other parts of the world, especially in the Southern Hemisphere and Asia, ministry as an entire way of life remains more integral and unified.[23] The churches of the North have much to learn from the churches of the South and East about validating and equipping all the baptized for their vocations in daily life. Still, even in those contexts, there is a tendency to reduce Christian ministry to the work of the institutional church.

The primary vocation of Christians is to live out the covenant God in Christ made with them at baptism: "to live among God's faithful people, to hear the word of God and share in the Lord's supper, to proclaim the good news of God in Christ through word and deed, to serve all people, following the example of Jesus, and to strive for justice and peace in all the earth."[24] Luther explains,

> For thus it is written in 1 Peter 2, "You are a chosen race, a royal priest-hood, and a priestly royalty." Therefore, we are all priests, as many of us as are Christians. But the priests as we call them, are ministers chosen from among us. All that they do is done in our name; the priesthood is nothing but a ministry. This is what we learn from 1 Corinthians 4: "This is how one should regard us, as servants of Christ and stewards of the mysteries of God."[25]

At the time of the Reformation, the universal priesthood was a radical claim about the equal status of all believers before God based on baptism. It was designed to overcome the dependency of the laity on the ministrations of a clerical hierarchy.

One problem with contemporary references to "the priesthood of all believers" is that the term itself now infers that to have real status as a minister one should become a "priest"—that is, an ordained pastor. Such a notion becomes another facet of the churchification of Christian ministry. In this way, speaking today about the "priesthood" of all believers has itself become problematic. The metaphor of "priesthood" can perpetuate a clerical misunderstanding of Christian vocation in the world—that is, real ministry is what "priests" (clergy) do.

Although Luther sought to reconfigure the late-medieval priesthood in relation to the priesthood of all believers, the practice of the Reformation churches has never adequately delivered the potency of this proposal. How might we reimagine the meaning of the universal "priesthood" by interpreting it as the "neighborliness" (*diakonia*) of all believers?[26] The neighborliness of all believers builds on the original intention of the priesthood of all believers concept but emphasizes the equal status of all believers, specifically focused on the service of neighbors. All believers in Christ are equally called to serve the neighbors God gives them in their respective spheres of influence.[27]

Affirming baptism as the primary ordination lends significance and status to all the baptized as ministers of the gospel of Jesus Christ. This should not be construed as a threat to the value of the pastoral ministry of word and sacrament. Rather, it provides the theological framework according to which pastors can serve in life-giving partnership with all members of the body of Christ. Ordained ministers serve word and sacrament through preaching, teaching, worship leadership, and pastoral care in order that the baptized are set free by the gospel of Jesus Christ *from* all that holds them captive and free *for* serving all the neighbors God gives them in the arenas of daily life. Moreover, it reminds pastors of the several roles and responsibilities they are called to serve in each arena of daily life beyond their pastoral service.

The ministry of deacons can serve as a catalyst to the revitalization of the neighborliness of all believers. Deacons exercise "word and service" ministry on behalf of the church. This ministry involves the proclamation and teaching of the Word of God and service to the neighbor in particular areas of specialization. Deacons perform a twofold service in the life of the church: (1) offer their own gifts in service to neighbors in their particular areas of specialization and (2) serve as a catalyst in the life of the church in order that all the baptized are equipped and empowered for ministries of word and service in every arena of daily life.

Worship Practices as Life Practices

Christians have a difficult time making connections between the things we do at worship and the things we are called to do when we leave the church building after worship.[28] The gulf between sanctuary and street is another sign of the disease of churchification. In reality, however, everything we do at worship is directly related to forming us for a way of life as Christian people in the world. As we participate in liturgy, we are not only worshipping God but also engaging in patterns that immerse us in the person and way of Jesus Christ himself, who makes us members of the body of Christ and engraves upon us Christ's very own character.

To grasp how worship practices are truly life practices, we need to begin with a very basic conviction: *God in Christ by the power of the Holy Spirit is the Primary Actor when we gather for worship.* When we define *liturgy* as "the work of the people," it is easy for us to lose sight of the most important Lutheran conviction informing our theology of worship. "We" are not the primary actors when we gather for worship; instead, God in Christ is the Primary Actor at worship who is "doing something to us." Worship is less about what we are doing for God and far more about how God is forming our character as the body of Christ in the world.

As we immerse ourselves in the worship practices of the liturgy, the Spirit forms us for specific Christian life practices in the world. Through these worship practices, God etches upon us the character of Jesus Christ and sends us to live out Christ's character in our relationships with others in our daily lives. Repetition of the distinctive parts of the liturgy imprints upon us both a way of being and a way of serving the neighbors God gives us in the various arenas of our daily lives: family/home, work/school, and the public world.

To see what God is up to at worship, it is useful to think carefully about each element of the worship service and make explicit how each of these worship practices is formation for life practices. Confession and absolution of sins, for example, is not merely a transaction between the worshipper and God. Rather, we learn through the worship practice of confession and absolution to live our lives according to the pattern of admitting our own faults and seeking reconciliation with our neighbors. We sing hymns of praise not only to honor God but in order that our entire lives be acts of praise. We receive God's peace by praying the Kyrie and by passing the peace in order that our lives conform to Christ's way of peace in all our relationships.

We hear God's Word and its proclamation as law and gospel that we become people dwelling in God's Word as the most important instruction (torah) for our lives. We confess creeds as declarations of the core convictions for which we live and for which we would be willing to die. We pray intercessions not only to ask God to intervene in the lives and concerns for which we pray; rather, these intercessions become our own mission statements. The things for which we pray are the very things to which we are to devote our own energy and effort. We receive an offering, which is to be understood as a sign that we intend to offer our bodies as a living sacrifice to God, which is our spiritual worship (Rom 12:1–2).

We share the Lord's Supper, saying that this is a meal in the name of Christ Jesus where all are welcome and where there is enough for all. Here we are formed as people who extend radical hospitality and share generously what we have with others in need. Luther says,

> Thus by means of this sacrament, all self-seeking love is rooted out and gives place to that which seeks the common good of all; and through the

change wrought by love there is one bread, one drink, one body, one community. This is the true unity of Christian[s].[29]

At the conclusion of worship, we receive a blessing and are sent. As you have been formed by these practices of worship, now live your lives according to these very patterns! At worship, we are formed as the body of Christ with the character of Jesus Christ engraved upon us by these practices of worship.[30] The practices we repeat at worship are the habits—a way of life—that shape our very identity as members of the body of Christ. Go in peace as the body of Christ: serve the Lord, share the good news, remember the poor!

The Nicene Creed names four characteristics by which the church is known: one, holy, catholic, apostolic. Normally as we reference these "marks" we think exclusively about the internal constitution of the church. These marks have been understood as ways the church is called to be true to its own identity—for example, ecumenical engagement as a sign of unity, church discipline as a sign of holiness, relating to other churches across time and space as a sign of catholicity, and faithfulness to biblical tradition as a sign of apostolicity.

Our neighbors, however, need these marks of the church to be lived out not only internally within the church but also externally—for the sake of the world. What would it mean to turn these ancient marks of the church inside out? Suddenly, the character of the body of Christ takes on new vitality for loving neighbors.

Oneness as a distinguishing character mark of the church comes to expression as the body of Christ gives itself to serve as a force for reconciliation and peacemaking in a world where estrangement and violence threaten to destroy the fabric of human community. Being body of Christ means praying, learning, and embodying "the things that make for peace" (Luke 19:42).

Holiness as a character mark of the church means engagement by the body of Christ in the work of social justice. Social holiness, following in the way of Jesus, entails feeding the hungry, caring for the sick, casting out evil spirits, radical hospitality to strangers, giving shelter to the homeless, and visiting prisoners (Matt 25:31–40).

Catholicity, as a character mark urgently needed in our times, involves the understanding that human beings are made of the selfsame material stuff (elements) as all the rest of God's creation. Human destiny is entirely dependent on the wellness of creation. Earth, water, sky, and all flora and fauna are also neighbors God has given us to love in the spirit of the Great Commandment (Matt 22:34–40).

Apostolicity as a character mark summons the body of Christ to vigilance in respecting and defending the inherent dignity of every person, who is created in God's image and for whom Jesus Christ died, without any exceptions. The apostolic imperative means we view every human being as someone precious to God, someone whose human rights are worth defending for Jesus's sake (Matt 11:28–30).

These four marks, which distinguish the character of Jesus Christ existing as community, constitute what it means for the body of Christ to live out our baptismal vocation for the sake of the neighbors God gives us in the arenas of our daily lives. At worship, we put on "the mind of Christ" (cf. Phil 2:5) and are formed as disciples in the way of Jesus. Being the body of Christ today means engaging in life-giving relationships with others and with creation as *shalom* church, embodying these character marks of the collective person Jesus Christ for the life of the world.

Here we draw an explicit connection between baptismal vocation and a theology and ethics of the cross (see chapter 7).[31] Jesus calls us to costly discipleship in the arenas of daily life: "If any want to become my followers, let them deny themselves and take up their cross and follow me" (Mark 8:34). Loving neighbors and loving creation mean entering the suffering of this world and taking the suffering of neighbors upon ourselves toward God's mending of creation (*tikkun olam*). Costly grace!

Fulfilling the Reformation Promise by Revitalizing the Universal Priesthood

For Luther, "faith is a living, daring confidence in God's grace so certain that you could stake your life on it one thousand times."[32] Charles Taylor comments on the Reformation heritage:

> The fullness of Christian life was to be found within the activities of this life, in one's calling and in marriage and the family. The entire modern development of the affirmation of ordinary life was, I believe, foreshadowed and initiated, in all its facets, in the spirituality of the Reformers.[33]

Ironically, however, Luther's affirmation of the universal priesthood largely has remained an unfulfilled promise of the Reformation, insofar as the churches themselves have perpetuated their own forms of ecclesial *incurvatus in se* and defended a clerical hierarchy instead of focusing their efforts on equipping the baptized for ministry in all arenas of daily life (Eph 4:11–16).

Bonhoeffer's call to costly discipleship finds its response when the costly grace of God in Jesus Christ sets us free to live out baptismal vocation for the sake of neighbors in our spheres of influence in daily life. Christian discipleship follows Jesus into the places he promises to meet us: yes, at worship in word and sacrament, yet also fully present in the relationships, roles, and responsibilities we have with the neighbors we encounter in everyday life (cf. Matt 25:34–40). How can we recover—again for the first time—the vocation of all the baptized serving their neighbors in families, at work and school, and for the common good, not only through what is organized by churches?

Justification by grace through faith in Christ alone must be inextricably paired with baptismal vocation as its matching twin. This involves no diminishment of the pure mercy of the gospel. The gospel of Jesus Christ in Luther's concept has always had freeing power—both freedom *from* and freedom *for*. "Freedom for" emerges because we have been justified by grace alone, based on the sheer gift to us of our belovedness for Christ's sake. The event of God's unconditional favor inherently turns us away from self-preoccupation, frees us, and turns us to care for the needs of neighbors and the integrity of creation. Justification and baptismal vocation belong together, just as the Great Commandment holds together love for God and love of neighbor (Matt 22:37–39).

To promote the vocation of the universal priesthood, a Life of Faith Initiative has been organized to provoke a culture change that frees us to make *service by the baptized in the arenas of daily life the central focus of the church's mission*.[34] This reform movement intends to reinvigorate focus on the ministry of all the baptized in many and varied forms of service to neighbors through the family, workplace, school, local community, and world. The vision of the Life of Faith Initiative affirms the following:

- We will learn to speak of "the expressions of the church" first as the people themselves, as well as the congregations, synods, denomination, and other agencies and institutions.
- We will be able to speak as easily and concretely about the ministry by all the baptized in daily life as we currently do about the ministry that happens in and through congregations and institutions.

- The center of gravity for our living out "missional church" will shift from what we do as the church gathered to what we do as the church scattered.
- The understanding of "ministry" will grow from "what pastors do" and "what we do as congregations" to include the love and service that is lived out in our everyday roles and relationships.
- We will become practiced at interpreting ministry in terms of the impact we are making in our homes, workplaces, schools, local communities, and around the world—not exclusively in terms of money received by the church or numbers of participants at church activities.
- All of us—from children to adults—will be able comfortably and confidently to speak and live the faith in our daily lives.
- Burdens will be lifted from pastors when they are no longer seen as the ones primarily responsible for the ministry of the congregation; they will find joy and fulfillment as ministry multiplies through the lives of all God's people.
- "Church" will no longer be in competition with the activities and responsibilities of members, and "ministry" will be expanded without asking people to add something more to their busy lives.
- The gathering rite in worship will be revised to better receive people after a week of ministry, allowing them to report "God sightings" and to receive forgiveness for failures; the sending rite will be expanded to better commission, equip, and send people for the coming week of ministry.
- When faith is connected to life, congregations will experience renewal in purpose and vitality.[35]

Just as Vatican II initiated an era of liturgical renewal during which sacramental ministry has been regaining its central place, today we need *a renewal of the ministry of the Word* in order that churches become teaching and learning communities where the people of God are equipped for the work of ministry in all their spheres of influence. We conclude with four theses on revitalizing the church through equipping the baptized for ministry in daily life:

1. God gives us neighbors to serve in the primary community of family. Two primary responsibilities for serving neighbors in families include

(a) providing basic *nutrition* and (b) providing healthy *nurture* and solid education, forming the next generation to attain capacity to care for others.

2. God gives us neighbors to serve in our daily work, no matter where that labor is lived out. Two primary responsibilities for serving neighbors in daily work include (a) securing *sufficiency* for human livelihood and (b) providing *significance* and meaning to life through the creative use of human gifts in the workplace.

3. God gives us neighbors to serve through religious institutions insofar as these institutions contribute to the common good. Two primary responsibilities for serving neighbors through religious institutions include (a) instilling a posture of *gratitude* in relation to life itself and (b) promoting *generosity* in relation to the needs of others.

4. God gives us neighbors to serve through engagement for the common good. Two primary responsibilities for serving neighbors in public life include (a) participation in the democratic process to implement strong and equitable *laws* that promote the good of all and (b) community organization and advocacy in political process, not merely to guarantee one's own self-interest, but to protect the needs of the most vulnerable, those whom Jesus named the *least*.[36]

If the universal priesthood is an unfulfilled promise of the Reformation, we must address this deficit by refocusing attention on equipping church members for Christian vocation, reclaiming baptism as ordination to ministry, as we serve the neighbors God gives us in the arenas of daily life. This is the heart of Lutheran ethics.

7

The Ethics of the Cross

JESUS SAYS, "IF ANY WANT TO become my followers, let them deny themselves and take up their cross and follow me" (Mark 8:34). One of the most distinctive contributions from the theology of Martin Luther for the Christian tradition is the theology of the cross. Theology of the cross originates from Luther's insight into where God chooses to be revealed: "through suffering and the cross."[1] Theology of the cross has consequential implications for ethics, authorizing an ethics of the cross. This is what Dietrich Bonhoeffer meant by the discovery of "the view from below."[2]

We need to recognize and challenge perilous false interpretations of the cross in Christian theology. Two false directions are especially misleading: triumphalism and trivialization. A triumphal interpretation twists the cross exclusively into a symbol of victory without attention to its original significance as an instrument of execution. This is the processional cross of the crusader and invader, or the cross embossed on the coat of arms of the monarch and empire. The triumphal cross subsumes the negative into the positive, transmuting the cross into a theology of glory. Nothing remains of the Crucified One after the resurrection victory.

Trivialization of the cross, by contrast, extracts from it all theological substance. "Bearing one's cross" is reduced to any unpleasant experience. Stubbing your toe or putting up with some ephemeral challenge becomes a cross to bear. Or the cross becomes a fashion accessory, like costume jewelry, or an icon in popular culture. The profundity of God's entrance into human suffering on the cross of Jesus Christ vanishes into superficiality. This chapter explores, by contrast, the contours of human suffering, the historical cross as a means of execution, the significance of the cross for ethical method, and the consequences of the cross for the Christian life.

Three Meanings of Human Suffering

As we explore an ethics of the cross in relationship to the reality of human suffering, it is crucial that we understand the suffering known to human beings is not all the same kind. Here we distinguish between three kinds of suffering: (1) the suffering that belongs to the finite human condition, (2) the suffering inflicted by some upon others and creation, and (3) the suffering we choose to take upon ourselves to participate in and share the suffering of others.

Existential Suffering

Type One suffering encompasses the suffering that is common to all humanity, which belongs to the finite human condition. Existential suffering encompasses a range of human experiences, including physical pain, emotional distress, mental illness, and spiritual despair. Physical pain relates to a range of experiences that include, for example, childbirth, growing, illness, bodily dysfunction, injuries, accidents, degenerative diseases, aging, and dying. Emotional distress ranges widely from feelings of fear, anxiety, loneliness, boredom, annoyance, jealousy, betrayal, confusion, disgust, regret, shame, guilt, worry, stress, and many others. The ability of human beings to identify and name with precision their own particular forms of emotional suffering reveals the extent to which the rich interior life of human beings fathoms the many facets of anguish.

Mental illnesses refer here to those conditions that are diagnosable and treatable by health professionals. Among the most common mental illnesses are depression and anxiety disorder. Others include bipolar disorder, schizophrenia, personality disorder, and eating disorder. Unlike physical illness, those with mental illnesses often have their suffering compounded by personal shame and social stigma. However, just as those with physical pain need to seek out medical help, those suffering from either emotional distress or mental illness deserve the same empathy and support from others to seek necessary treatment.

Finally, we include spiritual despair as an expression of Type One suffering. Despair is the condition of the soul that Søren Kierkegaard called "the sickness unto death."[3] The manifestations of spiritual despair include intense doubt and dread in facing the reality of death. This can include the conviction that one's spirit is beyond repair, worthless, or unforgivable. Spiritual despair also encompasses the condition of those who are unable to trust that they are forgiven or that the mercy of God in Christ could be true for them. It is important to include spiritual despair as a distinctive form of existential suffering, distinguishable from emotional distress or mental illnesses.

One of the most characteristic features of all forms of existential suffering is the isolation experienced by the person facing it. One "dimension of physical pain is its ability to destroy language, the power of verbal objectification, a major source of our self-extension, a vehicle through which the pain could be lifted out into the world and eliminated."[4] No one else can fully identify with the existential reality of suffering known only to the person facing it.

Preventable Suffering

By contrast, Type Two suffering refers to preventable suffering that human beings impose on one another and upon the world. A distinction here can be made between two forms of preventable suffering: those indignities experienced on an interpersonal level and those embedded in the social, economic, and political structures of society. When physical pain, emotional distress, mental illness, or spiritual despair is the consequence of identifiable human agency that could have been otherwise avoided, naming this reality is vital to its overcoming. Members of families, colleagues at work, peers at school, friends, acquaintances, people in the local community, or church members are among those who can inflict various kinds of harm on each other. Whereas interpersonal relationships inevitably are a source of existential suffering, it is an ethical imperative wherever possible to organize an intervention to change the circumstances leading to such causes of harm. For the moral injuries suffered, especially in interpersonal relationships, we enter the dynamics involved in an ethics of forgiveness (see the book's conclusion).[5]

Here we focus especially on how injustice has become embedded in social structures, referred to as "structural sin."[6] The social conditions under which marginalized people suffer are not merely a matter of fate. For example, we are called to reject every moral calculus that blames the victims of society's maldistribution of wealth as something they deserve due to their moral failure. While absolute social and economic equality may be an unrealizable ideal, utopian thought functions to provide an aspiration toward which social systems can seek approximation.[7] Historical analysis allows us to contrast how different societies establish distinctive political economies and legal structures that mitigate (or exacerbate) the distribution of wealth (e.g., through progressive taxation) and thereby increase (or interdict) access to food, housing, employment, and medical care as social goods.

Social disorder results from structural violence, economic injustice, ecological irresponsibility, and disrespect for human dignity. Structural violence is manifest, for example, in police brutality, fundamental inequities in the criminal justice system, surrogate warfare by states, engaging in warfare with disregard for political solutions, and "collateral damage" against civilians and creation in acts of war. The fundamental disparity of wealth causes economic injustice, for example, in the forms of hunger, homelessness, infant mortality, childhood stunting, homelessness, preventable diseases, inadequate medical care, and lack of basic social services.

Ecological irresponsibility is a correlate to established lifestyles of overconsumption that result, for example, in unnecessary products, excessive packaging, careless disposal of waste, inadequate recycling, water pollution, depletion of topsoil, overharvesting of natural resources, extinction of species, and the crisis of global heating. Disrespect for human dignity occurs in the harm done whenever the fundamental human rights of children, women, and men are not regarded and protected.[8] Particular attention must be given to safeguarding the rights of tribal, ethnic, racial, sexual, and other minority populations. In our age, these protections especially must encompass the increasing numbers of migrating people, whose dislocation has been caused exactly by the forms of structural violence, economic injustice, and ecological irresponsibility previously named. It is imperative that Type Two suffering, with its human causation, be strictly distinguished from those forms of existential suffering that are endemic to the human condition.

Sublime Suffering and the Way of the Cross

Type Three suffering encompasses all those instances of suffering that people voluntarily choose to take upon themselves to enter and share the burden of suffering experienced by others. This most deeply fulfills the saying of Jesus: "Let them deny themselves and take up their cross and follow me." While existential suffering is endemic to the finite human condition and preventable suffering is caused by human beings by either intent or thoughtlessness sublime suffering involves empathy, risk, and courage. While instances of sublime suffering are evident among those of diverse religious commitments or no religious commitment at all, this is the form of suffering most peculiar to Christian faith in following the way of Jesus. An ethics of the cross leads Christians to choose the way of the suffering to take up and bear the crosses of others.

When we consider the intercessions that we pray not only in our personal petitions but in our Christian assemblies, we are invited to enter the deep suffering of the world. This includes all those known to us by name who belong to or are connected to a given congregation—the sick, dying, grieving, injured, unemployed, or fearful ones—as well as for the needs of the entire world and all of creation. These intercessions are not merely a means to hand over to God things that are too difficult for us. Instead, our intercessions are a call to discipleship. If we dare to pray by name for the needs of the sick, grieving, or those in harm's way, the church of Jesus Christ is called to enter and share the burdens of these very people: sending messages of solidarity, visiting them, devising acts of kindness, providing material relief, and exercising agency to mitigate their suffering, whatever that might cost us. The integrity of the church depends on authenticity between what we profess—in this case, that for which we pray—and how we embody those words in deeds.

Correspondingly, if we pray for the needs of the world—the hungry, disaster victims, places ravaged by violence, soldiers serving in war zones, those harmed by racism or sexism—these are not mere pious wishes but a call to action. The body of Christ is called to analyze the complexity of the social issues related to these situations of suffering through study and to commit its energy and resources to engaging root causes to alleviate present suffering and reduce future suffering.[9] Rather than avoiding controversial topics—abortion, criminal justice, the death penalty, economics, genetics, health care, human sexuality, or racism—entering together into a process of ethical deliberation requires a level of risk that belongs to sublime suffering. Moral commitment is enhanced by communal deliberation and prepares the way for emerging discernment and consensus about collective action steps. Individuals remain free to follow their consciences regarding their own responses, which may range from loyal dissent to the option for more engaged activism.

To enter the suffering of others requires profound humility. Empathy begins by carefully listening to the stories and expressed needs of those directly affected. If failure to respond at all is a sin of omission, acting inappropriately can compound the very suffering we seek to relieve. Genuine solidarity depends

on establishing a climate of trust that continually is prepared to revise conclusions based on new evidence, especially honoring the perspective of the suffer-
ers. When it comes to sublime suffering for the sake of others, Luther's advice to
Philip Melanchthon bears repeating:

> If you are a preacher of grace, then preach a true, not a fictitious grace; if
> grace is true, you must bear a true and not a fictitious sin. God does not
> save people who are only fictitious sinners. Be a sinner and sin boldly, but
> believe and rejoice in Christ even more boldly. For he is victorious over
> sin, death, and the world.[10]

While we are always in danger of imperfection in our efforts at serving the suffering of others, the call to take up the cross and follow Jesus means taking the risk
and courage to act. This entails an act of Christian freedom for the sake of serving neighbors. Distinguishing among these three types of suffering—existential,
preventable, and sublime—prepares the way for exploring the divinely sublime
suffering of Jesus Christ crucified.

The Specificity of the Cross of Jesus Christ

Historically, the cross of Jesus Christ was an instrument of execution. On the
day we call Good Friday, no one—including perhaps Jesus himself—understood
the crucifixion as a salvific act of God. Jesus, their rabbi and friend, was condemned to execution by the Roman state. There were no reasons to believe that
this death would be remembered any more than the deaths of hundreds of other
criminals executed by this form of public spectacle. Jesus had been betrayed by
one and denied by another of his own disciples. Others went into hiding, fearing
that association with criminal Jesus could lead to their own arrest and demise.
Even the faithful women, some of whom stood by the cross, when they went
on the third day to the tomb brought the preparations to anoint a dead body. On
the day of his execution, there is compelling evidence that not even his closest
followers believed anything except this was the end of Jesus.

As to the form of his death, the cross was designed to inflict the maximum
of both physical pain and social humiliation. Crucifixion was a form of torture
and cruelty. The physical torment throughout the process was intense. Moreover, those executed on crosses were placed on public display, subjecting them

to public contempt and ridicule. The Passion Narratives witness to the cruelty inflicted on Jesus by the Roman authorities, soldiers, and crowd.

We fail to comprehend the finality of death by crucifixion as the end of Jesus whenever we rush to interpret the day of his death according to all we know through the lens of Easter. On Good Friday, worship services give us an opportunity to pause for one day to attend to the radical questions posed by this death. On Good Friday, we contemplate the finitude of human existence ultimately faced by each person. We have one day to reflect upon the radical question posed by Jesus himself: "My God, my God, why have you forsaken me?" (Mark 15:34).

This grave and radical question haunts human existence with the reality of death. How, then, shall we preach on Good Friday? How do we practice a pastoral care of the cross? How can Christian ministry address with profound seriousness the radical questions posed by Good Friday and Silent Saturday?[11] Where was God? Where was God when Jesus was crucified? Where is God when I experience profound suffering? Where is God when we participate in the deep suffering of others? Why does God continue to allow people to suffer death as by crucifixion?[12] Why does God remain silent to our pleas? Only by not giving answers too quickly, learning to live in the questions, can the church recover lost authenticity. Knowing how to cry while refraining from speaking prematurely accords with a theology of the cross. Having the discipline to remain silent belongs to an ethics of the cross. The crucifixion of Jesus hides God absolutely under the contradiction of death.

Good Friday was the day of Roman triumph. The accusation against Jesus was posted on the cross: "The King of the Jews" (Mark 15:26). Jesus and his fledgling kingdom movement had been crushed and would now be forgotten, just like the causes of all the others crucified by Rome. Paul, the earliest New Testament witness, best preserves the radicality of the cross in its first-century context: "The cross is foolishness" (1 Cor 1:18). Only when we recover the breathtaking finality of the cross of Jesus can we begin to fathom the reversal. In the words of the Apostles' Creed, Jesus "was crucified, died, and was buried; he descended to the dead."[13] Full stop. Silence. The end. Tomb closed.

Every salvific interpretation of the cross begins anew with the miracle of the resurrection. The resurrection announces a new day of creation in radical discontinuity from every day that had gone before. According to Jürgen Moltmann, "The salvific significance of the cross of Christ is only apparent in light of his resurrection from the dead. There is no salvific significance of the cross in isolation from his resurrection from the dead."[14] Only the encounter with the risen Jesus issued forth an entirely new rendering of the Hebrew Bible, as began along the road to Emmaus: "Then beginning with Moses and all the prophets, he interpreted to them the things about himself in all the scriptures" (Luke 24:27). It was after the resurrection that the words of the prophets were interpreted as foretelling of a crucified and risen Messiah, as in the oracles about a new covenant (Jer 31:31–34) or about the suffering servant (Isa 53:3–9). Only faith in the resurrection allowed apostles to describe the cross as "the power of God for salvation" (Rom 1:16). Every atonement metaphor that attributes positive value to the cross of Jesus occurs only subsequent to the new revelation by God through the resurrection: victory, sacrifice, expiation, forgiveness, revelation, or love. The resurrection gives rise to an entirely new and unprecedented epistemology of the cross. The invisibility of God in the human experience of the crucified Jesus gives way to hope for the sake of Christ's resurrection, hope for us that even in suffering one has not been abandoned by God.

Where God Chooses to Be Revealed

Given early Christian testimony to the resurrection of the crucified Jesus, the cross and resurrection became fused very early into one inseparable event: the cross-resurrection of Jesus Christ. Nevertheless, the Passion Narratives have preserved historical traces of the crucifixion as its own discrete moment in the story of Jesus of Nazareth. The risen Christ continues to bear the marks of the nails on his resurrected flesh: "Put your finger here and see my hands. Reach out your hand and put it in my side. Do not doubt but believe" (John 20:27). Lest the historical crucifixion of Jesus be minimized or even lost to theological reflection, this chapter argues for the imperative of retrieving the radical character of the cross for Christian ethics.

Luther retrieved the scandal of the cross for theology, especially through his presentation at the Heidelberg Disputation in 1518. His twenty-eight theological and twelve philosophical theses epitomize his attack on late-medieval scholastic theology. His critique of the role of human works and the exercise of free will in the attainment of salvation describes the character of the Wittenberg theology:

> 19. That person does not deserve to be called a theologian who perceives the invisible things of God as understandable on the basis of those things which have been made [Rom 1:20].

20. That person deserves to be called a theologian, however, who understands the visible and the "backside" of God seen through suffering and the cross.
21. A theologian of glory calls evil good and good evil. A theologian of the cross calls a thing what it actually is.
22. That wisdom which sees the invisible things of God in works as understood by human beings is puffed up, blinded, and hardened.[15]

Although these theses were articulated by Luther as a measure of theological precision ("the cross puts everything to the test"[16]), here we draw consequences for an ethics of the cross.

One of the most fascinating turns in recent theology is the proliferation of monographs in the English language devoted to the theology of the cross.[17] Two antecedents for this notable development were the publications of Jürgen Moltmann's *The Crucified God* in English translation in 1974 and Douglas John Hall's *Lighten Our Darkness: Toward an Indigenous Theology of the Cross* in 1976. Moltmann claimed, "All Christian theology and all Christian life is basically an answer to the question which Jesus asked as he died"[18] ("My God, why have you forsaken me?"). In examining what it means to have a crucified God, Moltmann juxtaposes Christology from below with particular experiences of human suffering in this world. This led him to give special attention to strategies that enhance both the psychological and political dimensions of human liberation. Moltmann's work resonates strongly with the concerns of liberation theology.

In reclaiming Luther's theology of the cross, Hall contextualized his concern by focusing on the meaning of the cross for an "officially optimistic society."[19] North American culture has been characterized by its persistent belief in human progress, its unbounded confidence in God's providential guidance of the US, and the expectation that hard work will lead every individual to success. By contrast, a theology of the cross allows for honesty about the reality and experience of negation that is suppressed and denied by an ideology of official optimism:

The theology of the cross is first of all a way of speaking about the character of God's entry into the sphere of human history. . . . It insists that God, who wills to meet us, love us, redeem us, meets, loves, and redeems us precisely where we are: in the valley of the shadow of death. . . . It insists that authentic happiness can only be found as we confront and enter into that which under the conditions of existence negates and dispels happiness.[20]

Both Moltmann and Hall seek to connect the profundities of the theology of the cross with the urgent questions facing humanity in our time.

Each of these recent works makes an original contribution to the interpretation and renewed vitality of the *theologia crucis* for our time.[21] At first, one can be struck by the diversity of claims made for the theology of the cross. Foundational are those works that explore the origins of cross theology in Paul and Luther exegetically and historically (Charles B. Cousar, Alister E. McGrath, Anna Madsen, and Dennis Ngien). In categorizing the others, one can distinguish three distinct approaches: (1) those that focus on the contrast with theologies of glory (Gerhard O. Forde and Vítor Westhelle), (2) those that criticize abuse of power (Winston D. Persaud, Mary Solberg, Deanna A. Thompson, and Theodore W. Jennings Jr.), and (3) those that intimate the inbreaking of God's kingdom (Douglas John Hall, David A. Brondos, Mark W. Thomsen, and John D. Caputo). We pray in the doxology to the Lord's Prayer: "For Thine is the kingdom, the power, and the glory." The theology of the cross functions in recent theology to insist that glory, power, and the kingdom itself belong only to God and God's crucified Son.

Why has so much attention been devoted to a theology of the cross in recent decades? In part, the answer relates to the conversion of the theology of the cross into an ethics of the cross. We offer two considerations. First, the enormity of human and global suffering has become ever more transparent through the instantaneous dissemination of information through electronic media. We are confronted immediately, overwhelmingly, and poignantly with profound human anguish and environmental disaster. The theology of the cross speaks eloquently to the depths of God's participation in the world's suffering and calls the church of Jesus Christ to solidarity with this suffering. Second, the urgent concern for the poor and the cry for social justice that emerged with liberation theologies are now finding expression through the advocates for an ethics of the cross. Contemporary interpreters of the theology of the cross increasingly link this theology with praxis for justice and peace. While in some respects an innovation, these ethical implications resonate with central biblical themes about bread for the hungry, care for the suffering, and meeting Christ in the least of these (Matt 25:31–46). The ethics of the cross through these innovative interpretations provide a compelling hermeneutic for engaging the meaning of Christian existence and peaceful coexistence in a multireligious and secular society.

Method in Liberation Theologies

The point of departure for liberation theologies is the experience of suffering, either by human beings or of creation. The work of liberation theologies begins wherever we hear a cry from those in pain or suffering: Why is this person screaming? Enrique Dussel says,

> One who hears the cry of pain is astonished because the scream resulting from a blow, a wound, or an accident indicates immediately not *something* but rather *somebody*. One who hears the cry of pain is astonished because the scream interrupts his commonplace and integrated world. The sound, the noise, produces a mental image of an absent-present somebody in pain. The hearer does not know as yet *what kind* of pain it is, nor the reason for the outcry. But the hearer will be disturbed until he knows who is crying out and why.[22]

Liberation theologies especially focus on preventable suffering, those forms of suffering that are avoidable and the consequence of structural sin. In Latin American liberation theology, the cry comes from the poor; in Black liberation theology, the cry derives from the structural racism deeply embedded in US history and society; in feminist theology, the cry arises against patriarchy; in Latinx liberation theology, it is the cry of alienated Latinx peoples; and in LGBTQIA+ liberation theologies, the cry is based on the experiences of lesbian, gay, bisexual, transgender, queer, and other persons not conforming to the established conventions of society regarding sexual orientation and/or gender binaries.

In Korean Minjung theology, the cry is from the socially and economically marginalized; in South Africa and Namibia, it is the cry of apartheid and its aftermath; in the Dalit theology of India, it is the cry of those oppressed under the caste system; in Palestinian liberation theology; it is the cry of political oppression related to dislocation from the land by settler colonialism; and in ecojustice theology, it is the cry of the planet caused by human interventions that erode and destroy the very conditions that make life possible. Every form of liberation theology begins inductively from the experiences of suffering people or a suffering creation.

Method for liberation theologies involves an action-reflection and praxis-oriented process in response to particular forms of suffering. This method typically consists of five moments: (1) the exploration of each particular expression of suffering based on oppression, (2) a prophetic critique of that condition based on biblical and theological precedents, (3) the use of social analysis to examine the causes of oppression and suffering, (4) the retrieval of biblical and theological materials to explore that suffering and seek to engage the particular oppression, and (5) advocacy for structural change toward a greater approximation of justice. Liberation theologies undertake intentional reflection upon concrete experiences of suffering, in which these five elements interact dynamically according to those forms of suffering and oppression specific to each group, attending to their historical experiences and context.

Liberation theologies are contextual theologies, emerging in specific locations and times. Their method aims to address specific forms of suffering and oppression by applying social analysis, which draws upon the wisdom of the sciences (especially the social sciences), and by employing biblical-theological reflection, which draws upon Scripture, church history, and theological resources. Because these theologies deal with the suffering and oppression of endangered groups, central topics for theological reflection include defining the human; analysis of sin—especially structural sin—that diminishes human worth and status; and advocating justice for the oppressed, including for creation itself.

Mary Solberg offers a usable description of method in liberation theology according to three movements, what she describes as "an epistemology of the cross":

1. Seeing or coming to know what is going on.
2. Recognizing and comprehending one's own relation to or involvement in what is going on.
3. Doing something about what is going on.[23]

The first step depends on having the eyes to see and ears to hear the experiences of suffering in the world around us. This involves an active searching for reliable information (beyond mass media accounts) about the economic and political events affecting people's lives and the well-being of creation (see chapter 2). One characteristic of consumer society is that we remain insulated from critical analysis of contemporary events. Many, if not most, influential news sources are driven by the self-interest of those who own these media outlets and by the advertisers whom the media aims to serve. Their influence on public opinion largely functions as a form of social control to pacify the public toward conforming to consumerism as a way of life. An ethics of the cross summons us to vigilance through active participation to discover what is going on in the world.

Second, there is the moment of ethical insight: I have responsibility for what is going on! This is a critical instance for democracy in crisis. Democracy depends on the practice of active participation by citizens. Increasingly, the control of the political process by elite economic interests—for example, through campaign contributions and the influence of lobbyists—is not only undermining the legitimacy of participatory democracy but subverting basic confidence that participation can make a difference.[24] This requires "faith" in democratic participation and advocacy as a means of social change (see chapter 8). The alternative is cynicism and despair about democratic institutions. Demoralizing of the public facilitates the consolidation of power by an economic oligarchy and the special interests that back them. If democratic involvement is to revive—and there are some encouraging signs—it begins with activism by concerned citizens at the grassroots. As change from the top down becomes increasingly less probable, change from the grassroots up becomes increasingly urgent. It is imperative we draw on inner courage to motivate ourselves to comprehend how we are implicated in what is going on and claim political agency.

Third, we are called to do something about what is going on. This involves strategizing for social change, organizing movements for social change, devising tactics for accomplishing social change, and engaging in strategic action to provoke social change. The value of building solidarity with others is crucial for both persistence and effectiveness. Today the possibility for organizing and building movements for effective social change is greatly enhanced by the same forms of social media used by others to provoke polarization and enervate energy for social change. It is essential for us to engage in spiritual practices to sublimate discouragement, despondency, frustration, and anger about the way things are by transmuting these into constructive energy on behalf of God's purpose of bringing forth *shalom* as life-giving relationships with others and creation.[25] Prayer, meditation, spiritual practices, and worship are means by which God transforms despair into hope toward active engagement in movements for social change. Solberg's threefold approach provides a practicable method that accords with the praxis orientation of liberation theologies.

Dietrich Bonhoeffer's experience of resistance to the principalities and powers in fascist Germany led him to discover "the view from below," which he commended to his circle of family and colleagues amid the political crisis of Nazism:

> There remains an experience of incomparable value. We have for once learned to see the great events of world history from below, from the perspective of the outcast, the suspects, the maltreated, the powerless, the oppressed, the reviled—in short, from the perspective of those who suffer. The important thing is neither that bitterness nor envy should have gnawed at the heart during this time, that we should have come to look with new eyes at matters great and small, sorrow and joy, strength and weakness, that our perception of generosity, humanity, justice and mercy should have become clearer, freer, less corruptible. We have to learn that personal suffering is a more effective key, a more rewarding principle for exploring the world in thought and action than personal good fortune.[26]

This claim by Bonhoeffer serves as a clarion call for righteous action in solidarity with suffering people and a suffering creation for us today. Bonhoeffer witnesses to an ethics of the cross in accordance with the invitation of Jesus to "take up your cross and follow me." We ask God for the wisdom and courage to pay attention to "the perspective of the outcast, the suspects, the maltreated, the powerless, the oppressed, the reviled" as a hermeneutic of the cross lends our lives meaning and purpose.

For Bonhoeffer, it was an ethics of the cross that led him to advocate early on for three forms of Christian political action in response to state injustice. First, the church was called to interrogate state injustice: "questioning the state as to the legitimate state character of its actions—that is, making the state responsible for what it does." Second, the church was obligated to help the casualties of injustice: "service to the victims of the state's actions. The church has an unconditional obligation toward the victims of the state's actions." And third, the church might be called to bring to a halt the machinery of injustice: "not just to bind up the wounds of the victims beneath the wheel but to seize the wheel itself. Such an action would be direct political action on the part of the church."[27] When he gave this address in 1933, Bonhoeffer could not yet imagine a fourth measured response that would later compel him and the conspirators to plan for the execution of a coup d'état.

An ethics of the cross summons disciples to enter into the complexities of a suffering world. The cross of Jesus Christ is the occasion for neither triumphalism nor trivialization. The cross was very intentionally the means of execution for a Roman criminal from whom one would expect to hear no more. Yet by the power of the resurrection, God created the world anew in Jesus Christ. Just as God chose to be revealed in the crucifixion, God now chooses to be disclosed in the suffering places of this world. Theologies of liberation take the suffering of human beings and of creation as the point of departure for theological reflection and ethical commitment.

We conclude this chapter with four convictions based on the ethics of the cross: (1) God especially chooses to be found in places of suffering, (2) much suffering in this world is caused by human beings and therefore preventable, (3) an ethics of the cross seeks to meet God in exactly those suffering places, and (4) the theologian of the cross joins in that suffering through advocacy and praxis.

8 Luther's Two Strategies and Political Advocacy

How might a Christian think theologically and ethically about participation in political advocacy? This question is especially urgent given the persistent—yet mistaken!—notion that separation of church and state precludes Christian involvement in the work of political advocacy. Employing Martin Luther's two kingdoms as a paradigm for interpreting his theology proves fruitful as a framework for understanding the dynamics of Christian political advocacy. To appropriate Luther's teaching, we first need to reinterpret Luther's two kingdoms teaching constructively as God's two strategies for ruling the world (building on chapter 4). Next, we clarify several misinterpretations and apparent contradictions in Luther's thought. Just as it has proven customary and insightful to distinguish between two uses of the law in Luther's writings, we also gain clarity about his understanding of righteousness, reason, will, and works by recognizing both a civil and a spiritual use of these key concepts. This chapter focuses on redefining these categories according to their differentiated use in the two distinctive strategies. Finally, this chapter draws conclusions for the work of political advocacy by contrasting religious identity politics with neighbor politics as alternative approaches by Christians.

Luther's Two Strategies and the Work of Advocacy

Although the usefulness of Luther's two kingdoms teaching has been severely challenged due to its tragic misinterpretations in the late nineteenth and twentieth centuries, especially in the Nazi period, it remains a constructive paradigm for understanding the dialectical character of Luther's thought.[1] As we saw earlier, one fundamental mistake involves the conventional notion that the "two" kingdoms refer to two separated realms of activity, often identified as the division between church and state.[2] Whereas separation of church and state refers constitutionally to the limitation placed upon government to impose religious beliefs on citizens, many Christians persist in thinking that the disestablishment clause means the church as church (and thereby Christians as Christians) should have nothing to do with politics. This poses questions and creates resistance among many church members about the legitimacy of the church's social teaching as a guide to political advocacy, particularly as it comes to expression in social statements.[3] By contrast, a dialectical interpretation of Luther's two kingdoms, understood as God's two strategies for ruling the world, distinguishes between but does not separate the interconnections between the two kingdoms (see chapter 4). Whereas it has been confusing to employ the spatial metaphor, "kingdom," to conceptualize Luther's proposal without thinking in terms of a separation of realms, the use of the term *strategies* is conducive for understanding that God can work in two distinguishable but interrelated ways.

Luther had a vivid imagination for how God was engaged in a battle with Satan for control of this world.[4] This is another challenging aspect of Luther's two strategies approach in a world where many no longer understand Satan as a personal figure against whom God contends in pursuing human allegiance. The reinterpretation of the principalities and powers in the New Testament can be of assistance for reclaiming the dynamism of Luther's theology in opposition to the influence of evil.[5]

According to Luther, God employs two distinct but interrelated strategies for extending God's kingdom. Elaborating on our earlier discussion, each strategy employs particular means to serve God's purposes. According to the right-hand strategy, God has accomplished salvation by the incarnation, death, and resurrection of Jesus Christ. Central to Luther's concept is that the work of Jesus Christ occurs according to justification by grace through faith. Salvation is entirely God's merciful work granted to sinners for Christ's sake alone. This gift is mediated through word and sacrament, the means of grace by which the Holy Spirit delivers Christ's real presence and the gifts that belong to Christ. Proclamation of the Word certainly includes the preaching and teaching of the church in the gathered assembly but also encompasses the verbal communication by church members who tell the promises of Jesus Christ to others in all their roles and relationships in life.[6] Holy Baptism and Holy Communion are sacraments by which Jesus Christ is really present to incorporate members into the body of Christ and to nourish with his body and blood those who partake of the meal.

For Luther, the central gift of the gospel of Jesus Christ is Christian freedom (see chapter 3). Jesus Christ grants believers *freedom from* everything that holds them in bondage. This means, according to *The Small Catechism*, that Jesus Christ sets believers free from all sins, from death, and from the power of the devil. Equally vital is understanding that Jesus Christ also grants believers *freedom for*! Although Christian existence always remains under the proviso of *simul justus et peccator* (simultaneously saint and sinner), Christian freedom means real freedom for service to the neighbors God gives us in this world, including creation itself as our neighbor. By the power of the Holy Spirit, working through the gospel as mediated by the means of grace, Christians are sent into the world to embody the neighborliness (*diakonia*) of all believers.[7] This sending propels the baptized to participate in God's right-hand strategy through evangelical listening and speaking the promises of Christ to others; it also sends Christians to participate in God's left-hand strategy for ruling the public world, the theme of this chapter.

God's left-hand strategy involves God's governing the public world through structures that serve to protect from harm and approximate justice, justice being the public form of love.[8] In the sixteenth century, Luther named three institutions established by God to order the world: family, church, and government. At that time, family encompassed not only familial relations but the family's economic livelihood. Given the demarcation between family and work after the Enlightenment, it is more useful today to think about four interrelated arenas of public responsibility by Christians: family, work, church as religious institution, and citizenship.

Christians are formed by worship and the narrative of Scripture to render service to neighbors in God's left-hand strategy (see chapter 6).[9] These neighbors include members of one's own family, persons served through relationships in the workplace as well as through the work itself, those whose lives are affected by involvements in one's local community, people impacted by the contributions of religious institutions to civil society, and those served by political advocacy for just legislation and policies. It is important to stress at this point that not only Christians serve neighbors through these arenas but rather God seeks to engage all people, whether religious or not, to serve neighbors through these arenas in the left-hand strategy. While Christians may be intentional about serving neighbors through these arenas, according to Luther, all people are serving neighbors in these capacities *whether they know it or not*, thereby doing God's will.

God's left-hand strategy aims at an ever-greater approximation of justice for the common good, evaluated by how the most vulnerable (e.g., the poor; ethnic, racial, and religious minorities; victims of violence; and endangered creation) are faring. This norm for evaluating political advocacy sets priorities in four arenas. The agenda of a *family politics* involves guaranteeing nutrition (food security) and nurture (strong public education) for the next generation. The agenda of an *economic politics* involves guaranteeing sufficient livelihood for all people and the significance of work in drawing upon people's abilities in a meaningful way. The *politics of religious institutions* involves instilling a sense of gratitude that leads to generosity on behalf of neighbors for the public good. The agenda of *political advocacy* involves activism in promoting laws that provide equity among all members of civil society and with particular attention to the well-being of the least. Good government must be measured by how those most endangered and marginalized, including creation itself, are treated.

Christians are called to work together and build coalitions with all those who share their commitments to the common good, whether those allies are Christians, members of other religious faiths, or neither. To clarify the dialectical relationship between God's right-hand spiritual and left-hand civil strategies, it is useful to contrast and distinguish how we understand varied human capacities in relation to each of these strategies. Therefore, it is useful to differentiate between not only two uses of the law from a Lutheran perspective, as has become customary, but also two uses of righteousness, reason, will, and works. Precision about these categories can assist in elucidating the responsibilities of Christian engagement in political advocacy.

Two Uses of the Law

As evidenced by standard interpretations of Luther's theology, it has become conventional to distinguish between a first civil use of the law and a second theological use. Bernhard Lohse makes the bold claim that "Luther is clearly the first in all of history of dogma and theology to view the law from the viewpoint of its uses, thus in its concrete function." Lohse analyzes Luther's twofold use of the law, which first appeared in his writings in 1522 and reached its most fulsome exposition in the Galatians lectures of 1531.[10] Lohse concisely summarizes,

> The two functions of the law are the "political" or "civic" and the "theological." Here too there is a profusion of formulas and terms. By means of the political use, external order on earth is to be maintained, and peace and the securing of justice preserved. The law has also the task of inculcating the divine commandments and of instructing the consciences. It also furnishes the needed means by which to punish evildoers. The order established by the political use of the law is affected through the offices of the temporal authorities, of parents, of teachers, and of judges, instituted by God for this purpose. If the law in its political use is obeyed, then an "external," "civic" righteousness is achieved, to which Luther assigned the highest value. . . . The "theological" use comprises the authentic task of the law. It is, so to speak, the law in its spiritual sense. This use serves to show persons their sin, to "convict" them of sin. . . . The law "accuses," "horrifies," indicating that owing to their guilt humans are not what they should be before God.[11]

Paul Althaus interprets the two uses of the law in a corresponding manner, as does Oswald Bayer.[12]

The distinction between the two uses of the law is directly related to Luther's theological paradigm of the two kingdoms—or, more precisely, two strategies. Due to the prevalent misinterpretation of the two kingdoms as separate realms or arenas dividing church from public life, which has led tragically to political quietism (e.g., the failure of Christian resistance to fascism in Nazi Germany), a more dynamic approach appropriates the two kingdoms as two distinctive yet complementary forms of divine activity in the world. God engages ambidextrously with both hands to rule the world with the gospel of Jesus Christ according to the right-hand spiritual strategy and by means of the structures and institutions of public life according to the left-hand civil strategy.

Two Uses of Righteousness: Civil and Alien

The two strategies paradigm frames the distinction in Luther's theology between the two uses of the law. The first use of the law functions as God's way of ordering and structuring the world in the left-hand strategy, while the second use of the law functions to expose and condemn sin as preparation for the proclamation of the gospel in the right-hand strategy. However, it is equally compelling to construe other central categories in Luther's thought according to their contrasting uses and functions in relation to the two strategies. Thereby, Luther distinguishes two contrasting forms of righteousness. In God's right-hand spiritual strategy, the only righteousness that matters is the alien righteousness that belongs to the sinner through justification by grace alone through faith alone in Christ Jesus. Althaus writes,

> The righteousness of Christ is imputed to the sinner. God sees the sinner as one with Christ. He forgives his sin and considers the sinner to be righteous for Christ's sake. Thus the righteousness granted to the sinner is not his own produced by himself but an "alien" righteousness belonging to Jesus Christ.[13]

By the work of Christ, the sinner receives the alien righteousness of Jesus Christ as pure gift (*extra nos*) and for Christ's sake through faith becomes truly righteous before God.

Civil righteousness, by contrast, is that form of righteousness that all persons perform in relationship to their neighbors in God's left-hand civil strategy. Non-Christians also have the capacity to engage in civil righteousness in service to neighbors in their families, workplaces, and public lives. God structures and orders daily life through those who live out their roles with responsibility to care for others as neighbors. Although this form of righteousness may play a secondary role in Luther's thought, it remains an essential concept for accomplishing God's purposes of protecting and preserving the world. Althaus describes with reference to Luther,

> Thus this outward righteousness is indeed considered less valuable than the true righteousness of the Christian. However, it does have positive value, for it says "that in his station everyone should do his duty." If people were seriously concerned about this secular righteousness, "there would be no rascality or injustice, but sheer righteousness and blessedness on earth."[14]

Human ethical capacity, even under the condition of sin, can and does contribute a measure of civil righteousness to the created world according to the left-hand civil strategy. Civil righteousness finally remains an approximation of God's created purposes, however, due to the pervasiveness of human waywardness, which becomes manifest not only in the personal realm but as structural sin.

The distinction between the first and second uses of righteousness in Luther's thought is fruitful for elucidating both the centrality of the work of Christ in imputing alien righteousness according to God's spiritual strategy and the ethical responsibility of human beings to contribute to public righteousness for their neighbors according to God's civil strategy. Both forms of righteousness have their proper locations and uses in Lutheran ethics.

Two Uses of Reason: Gift and "Harlot"

Luther famously asserted against reason: "And what I say about the sin of lust, which everybody understands, applies also to reason; for reason mocks and affronts God in spiritual things and has in it more hideous harlotry than any harlot."[15] The standard view regarding Luther's understanding of human reason is largely informed by his polemic in *The Bondage of the Will*. Here Luther, in defense of the doctrine of justification by pure grace through faith in Jesus Christ, takes an aggressive stance against the synergism of late-medieval scholastic theology, even as represented by a moderate figure like Erasmus. Reason confronts its absolute limit in relation to what God has revealed in Jesus Christ for accomplishing salvation. God's right-hand spiritual strategy has been fulfilled neither through human reasoning nor by the cooperation of the human will but solely by God's inscrutable action in the death and resurrection of Jesus Christ. Luther writes,

> Ask reason herself whether she is not convinced and compelled to confess that she is foolish and rash in not allowing the judgment of God to be incomprehensible, when she admits that everything else divine is incomprehensible. . . . We cannot for a while believe that he is righteous, even though he has promised us that when he reveals his glory we shall all both see and feel that he has been and is righteous.[16]

Human beings do not cooperate with God in the attainment of eternal salvation. To claim a human role, even a minor one, would be an affront to the majesty and glory of God, who assumes sole responsibility for all matters pertaining to human redemption. As Paul attests, "For the message of the cross is foolishness to those who are perishing, but to us who are being saved it is the power of God" (1 Cor 1:18 NKJV).

Whereas Luther takes a decidedly negative stand against the use of reason in the right-hand spiritual strategy, his writings demonstrate the positive and valued use of reason through human engagement with creation according to the left-hand civil strategy:

> It is certainly true that reason is the most important and the highest rank among all things and, in comparison with other things of this life, the best and something divine. It is the inventor and mentor of all the arts, medicines, laws, and of whatever wisdom, power, virtue, and glory men possess in this life. By virtue of this fact it ought to be named the essential difference by which man is distinguished from the animals and other things. Holy Scripture also makes it lord over the earth.[17]

Luther himself was an educator, providing materials for the instruction of the church at every level, including *The Small Catechism* and *The Large Catechism*. Consequently, Lutheran theology always has placed a high value on the contribution of human reason for understanding the nature of the world.[18] Moreover, the Lutheran churches have dedicated themselves to institutions of higher learning, understanding education as an indispensable contribution to civil society.[19]

Perhaps the most compelling reference by Luther to the gift of reason within the left-hand civil strategy was his testimony before the emperor at the Diet of Worms on April 18, 1521:

> Since then your serene majesty and your lordships seek a simple answer, I will give it in this manner, neither horned nor toothed: Unless I am convinced by the testimony of Scriptures or by clear reason (for I do not trust either in the pope or in councils alone, since it is well known that they have often erred and contradicted themselves), I am bound by the Scriptures I have quoted and my conscience is captive to the Word of God. I cannot and I will not retract anything, since it is neither safe nor right to go against conscience.[20]

Here Luther not only demonstrates the practice of sound reasoning through the logic of his statement but grounds his own reasoning on the two sources of authority most befitting each of the two strategies: scriptural authority in the right-hand spiritual strategy and reason as authority in the left-hand civil strategy. Not only Scripture but reason has its proper use, for example, when standing before the emperor's tribunal.

Two Uses of the Will: Limited within Creation and in Bondage regarding Salvation

Not only through the exercise of reason but also in the exercise of the will is it fruitful to distinguish between two uses. Regarding the saving work of God in Jesus Christ according to the right-hand spiritual strategy, the will is totally and completely in bondage and of no use:

> For my own part, I frankly confess that even if it were possible, I should not wish to have free choice given to me, or to have anything left in my own hands by which I might strive toward salvation. . . . But now, since God has taken my salvation out of my hands into his, making it depend on his choice and not mine, and has promised to save me, not by my own work or exertion but by his grace and mercy, I am assured and certain both that he is faithful and will not lie to me, and also that he is too great and powerful for any demons or any adversities to be able to break him or to snatch me from him.[21]

Again, it is clearly demonstrated that neither human righteousness nor reason nor will has anything constructive to contribute to the winning of salvation according to the right-hand spiritual strategy. God alone secures salvation in Christ Jesus without any cooperation on the part of human beings.

Throughout his writings, Luther is generally skeptical about the human exercise of the will, which is affected always by the power of sin. In his argument with Erasmus in *The Bondage of the Will*, however, he does allow for some exercise of free choice in relation to human involvements in the left-hand civil strategy:

> But if we are unwilling to let this term go altogether—though that would be the safest and most God-fearing thing to do—let us at least teach men to use it honestly, so that free choice is allowed to man only with respect

to what is beneath him and not what is above him. That is to say, a man should know that with regard to his faculties and possessions he has the right to use, to do, or to leave undone, according to his own free choice, though even this is controlled by the free choice of God alone, who acts in whatever way he pleases. On the other hand, in relation to God, or in matters pertaining to salvation or damnation, a man has no free choice, but is a captive, subject and slave either of the will of God or the will of Satan.[22]

In relation to the created order, the human will can play a useful role "with respect to what is beneath him." Once again, the two strategies framework provides a constructive paradigm for distinguishing between two contrasting uses of the will in Luther's theology.

Two Uses of Works: For the Neighbor and Works Righteousness

Finally, with regard to Luther's interpretation of human works, there is a clear difference between works righteousness in the right-hand spiritual strategy and the performance of works for the sake of the neighbor in the left-hand civil strategy. The Reformation was launched in protest of the late-medieval theological paradigm that promoted the performance of religious rituals as the way to earn status before God. Luther's "95 Theses" exposed the fallacies of a theological system that assigned merit to sinners through the trade and sale of papal indulgences, which were understood as good works.[23] Luther roared against every "claim to be justified by works, whatever their character":

Since faith alone justifies, it is clear that the inner man cannot be justified, freed, or saved by any outer work or action at all, and that these works, whatever their character, have nothing to do with this inner man. On the other hand, only ungodliness and unbelief of heart, and no outer work, make him guilty and a damnable servant of sin. Wherefore it ought to be the first concern of every Christian to lay aside all confidence in works and increasingly to strengthen faith alone and through faith to grow in the knowledge, not of works, but of Christ Jesus. . . . No other work makes a Christian.[24]

This quote from *The Freedom of a Christian* elucidates Luther's first thesis that "a Christian is a perfectly free lord of all, subject to none."[25] We are justified by faith alone in Jesus Christ, not by works of law. In the right-hand spiritual strategy, faith, trusting in the saving work of Christ, is the only good work.[26]

Luther, however, does preserve an essential place for the performance of good works—not for earning merit from God toward salvation but as a service to the well-being of the neighbor. This is the meaning of Luther's second thesis in his treatise on Christian freedom: "A Christian is a perfectly dutiful servant of all, subject to all."[27] Luther continues,

> Lastly, we shall also speak of the things which he does toward his neighbor. A man does not live for himself alone in this mortal body to work for it alone, but he lives also for all men on earth; rather, he lives only for others and not for himself. . . . Therefore he should be guided in all his works by this thought and contemplate this one thing alone, that he may serve and benefit others in all that he does, considering nothing except the need and advantage of the neighbor.[28]

Luther's theology retains a prominent place for the performance of good works, not in relation to God's saving work in Christ, but as a vital aspect of God's left-hand civil strategy through service to our neighbor. Good works proper, as described in the *Treatise on Good Works*, are those due to others according to the Ten Commandments, particularly in the Second Table of the Law.[29] Once again regarding the meaning of works, Luther distinguishes two uses in accordance with the two divine strategies.

Luther's Two Strategies and Political Advocacy

Political advocacy refers to efforts by the church to change societal structures, promote economic policies, and enact legislation that is consistent with God's purpose of bringing forth the kingdom—that is, *shalom*. The charters of organizations like the Fellowship of Reconciliation, Bread for the World, 350.org, and Amnesty International provide reference points for this distinctive type of political advocacy. Denominational advocacy efforts with regard to racism, sexism, heterosexism, poverty, hunger, homelessness, violence, war, arms proliferation, prisons, capital punishment, environmental concern, and other issues belong to Christian participation in God's left-hand strategy. Likewise, congregation members may wish to raise their voices on behalf of a particular cause that entails changing societal structures.

Controversy over the place of political advocacy in the church's outreach has many causes. Fundamental to the debate are conflicting views about the proper relationship of church and state, in particular the role of church in society. According to a very popular view, the primary role of the church has been *privatized* as it ministers to the spiritual needs of people through worship and pastoral care, with a secondary role of offering *charitable assistance* to people in need. The ministry of the church belongs to the private realm of individuals and families who choose to participate in it. The mediation of the church's ministry is highly individualized, based on concern for the spiritual welfare of persons and helping with their individual needs. In this view, the ministry of the church is relegated to the private sphere. It must remain separated from matters debated in the public square, except when those debates threaten the rights of the church's functioning in the spiritual realm belonging to it. Since the nineteenth century, the church has been subject increasingly to the privatization of religion, relegated to a delimited compartment of life and leading to the quietism of the church in public affairs.[30]

A second and dramatically contrasting approach for relating church and state has been taken by the so-called Christian right.[31] This approach can be characterized as a form of *religious identity politics*. According to this approach, the church is called to be vigilant in ordering society according to Christian principles. In the Bible, God has revealed the truth about key social issues (e.g., regarding abortion, marriage, homosexuality, or the teaching of evolution). Therefore, it becomes the responsibility of Christians to become involved in the political process to ensure that the "Christian" position on each of these issues prevails. Churches operating according to particular "religious identity politics" issues direct their membership about how to vote not only on those issues but sometimes also for particular political parties and candidates, whom they reckon will offer the best support for their agenda. These churches also actively advocate with legislators according to their established agenda. The goal is to implement legislation and policies based on their interpretation of God's will revealed in the Bible.

In US society, there are many Christians who understand the relationship of church and state according to this paradigm. This approach has had significant influence on the outcome of key elections. This leads many politicians to calculate how they can best appeal to the power of this voting bloc. At the same time, the assertiveness of the Christian right has led to a significant backlash by those who reason differently and come to different conclusions about particular issues. This backlash comes not only from many Christians but especially from those not affiliated with the church. Many secular citizens and those from other faith traditions wrongly assume that all Christians share this approach to politics. This complicates the challenge facing Christians who operate out of other paradigms for relating church and state, such as God's two strategies as developed in this book.

Political advocacy belongs to the responsibility of the baptized, according to the left-hand strategy of God, both through their personal initiative as citizens and through the collective efforts of the institutional church in its political advocacy as public church. However, a major difference exists between the political approach of the Christian right and advocacy according to God's left-hand strategy. In contrast to religious identity politics, Christians are called to engage in what may be characterized as *neighbor politics*. Neighbor politics is undertaken in consonance with the political use of the law, civil righteousness, reason, will, and good works as God's gifts for analyzing and understanding the world in God's left-hand strategy.

When it comes to political involvement by Christians, rather than basing political judgments on explicitly biblical warrants or religious arguments, effective Christian participation in politics requires that Christians employ reasonable arguments that are intelligible and coherent to all citizens, not just to those who share Christian theological commitments. Christians are to employ language and reasoning that are accessible to all. They are to direct their attention, above all, to the well-being of neighbors in political advocacy, reasoning according to what contributes to the common good of society, with particular concern for those who are suffering under current laws, policies, and programs. While this does not preclude references to biblical or theological authority, such appeals are most appropriate when they strengthen arguments and rhetoric that are publicly accessible.

Neighbor politics by Christians differs dramatically from the religious identity politics of the Christian right, which is heavily laden with biblical and religious arguments and whose goal is to impose its religious conclusions on the whole society. By contrast, while motivated by Christian faith—freed by the gospel of Jesus Christ for neighbor love—Christians participate in God's left-hand strategy by speaking out and engaging in the political process as citizens who advocate for the well-being of the neighbor, using reasonable arguments that appeal to the consciences and common sense of others, building coalitions wherever possible with those who share a common vision, and avoiding special pleading based on a "Christian" agenda narrowly understood. While Christians certainly base their political involvements on their faith—drawing upon the significance of Scripture and theology for their convictions—when they move into the public arena with a neighbor politics, they privilege reasoning and explanations accessible to all. This approach is dramatically different from the religious identity politics of the Christian right, which on key issues funds its agenda as the theocratic imposition of its religious agenda on society.

This chapter reclaims Luther's two strategies as a comprehensive paradigm for interpreting the work of political advocacy by Christians. It is fruitful to identify and distinguish for Lutheran ethics not only a first and second use of the law, as has become conventional in Lutheran theology, but also first and second uses of righteousness, reason, will, and works. The dialectical use of these concepts is elucidated with reference to the fundamental paradigm of God's two complementary and dialectical strategies for ruling the world. According to the second use of these categories in relation to the right-hand spiritual strategy, they are precluded as threatening divine sovereignty in the securing of salvation through Jesus Christ and procuring the gifts of the forgiveness of sins, deliverance from the power of the devil, and eternal life. However, according to the first use of these categories in the left-hand civil strategy, each of these human capacities has a necessary, though circumscribed, role in the work of political advocacy toward the approximation of the common good and preservation of God's creation. Through the use of law, righteousness, reason, will, and works in the left-hand civil strategy, this paradigm offers a constructive foundation for Lutheran ethics in the work of political advocacy, an approach that is in dramatic contrast to the religious identity politics manifest in other prominent forms of political engagement by Christians, especially that of the religious right in the US.

Conclusion

The Ethics of Forgiveness

ALL OF HUMAN LIFE, INCLUDING THE ethical life, inhabits the tragic condition of sin. As articulated in the order of confession, "We confess that we are captive to sin and cannot free ourselves. We have sinned against you in thought, word, and deed, by what we have done and by what we have left undone. We have not loved you with our whole heart; we have not loved our neighbors as ourselves."[1] According to Paul Tillich, our lives become subject to "demonic" distortion whenever our minds submit to the power of elements that aspire to "grasp the center of the rational self and destroy it."[2] The demonic involves the distortion of what God created as good and comes to expression in sinful thoughts, words, and deeds.

Sin begins with distorted thinking, is unveiled by how we speak, and manifests itself in human actions at both the personal and societal levels.[3] The reality of sin originates in how we may think about our own lives in either self-aggrandizing or self-deprecating ways. It furthermore encompasses how we come to think in biased ways about others, including the company of creation. Common cognitive distortions include filtering out the positive to focus on the negative, polarization, overgeneralizing, catastrophizing, or blaming.[4] Our sinful thinking contrasts with the Pauline appeal to "let the same mind be in you that was in Christ Jesus" (see Phil 2:5–8).

The sinful distortions within our minds and thinking become articulated in how we speak. According to James 3:5–10a,

> So also the tongue is a small member, yet it boasts of great exploits. How great a forest is set ablaze by a small fire! And the tongue is a fire. The tongue is placed among our members as a world of iniquity; it stains the whole body, sets on fire the cycle of nature, and is itself set on fire by hell. For every species of beast and bird, of reptile and sea creature, can be tamed and has been tamed by the human species, but no one can tame the tongue—a restless evil, full of deadly poison. With it we bless the Lord and Father, and with it we curse those who are made in the likeness of God. From the same mouth come blessing and cursing.

Through our speech, we misrepresent the world, its creatures, and our human neighbors. Finally, sin becomes embodied in destructive actions against the self, other people, and the entire creation. Structural sin refers to the ways human sinfulness has become embedded in public procedures and policies and by how they are enforced. Structural sin permeates legal, medical, educational, economic, political, religious, and all other systems.

Of all Christian teachings, the doctrine of sin has the most empirical evidence to substantiate its validity. As Jeremiah contended, "The heart is devious above all else; it is perverse—who can understand it?" (Jer 17:9). Or as Paul declared, "All have sinned and fall short of the glory of God" (Rom 3:23). Given what we observe in private life, institutionally, and in the public realm, *we should never underestimate the power of sin, either in ourselves or in others.* Human creativity exerts itself in astounding ways for self-serving and harmful purposes.

God has instituted the left-hand strategy to safeguard the world and its creatures from the damaging effects of human sin, including the ways sin becomes manifested in societal structures. The natural law tradition affirms not only that are there universal laws undergirding the physical world, but universal ethical laws also govern the moral universe. The natural law originates from the first commandment: "You shall have no other gods before me" (Exod 20:3). God has established life-giving values by which we are to order the moral universe, lest human society disintegrate. While the Roman Catholic moral tradition has an extensive history and practice of basing ethical arguments on core principles from the natural law, Protestant traditions often leave natural law foundations and arguments more implicit than explicit, especially under the sway of postmodern constructivist epistemologies. It is important to remember that Martin Luther himself held that the Ten Commandments themselves, specifically the Second Table of the Law, testify to the existence of natural law as "written on their heart."[5]

The instruments God employs to implement the natural law and to limit the power of human sin take several expressions. First, God has given human beings a conscience by which to engage in self-examination and criticize one's own behavior. Second, God locates our lives in community with other people, who have responsibility to call us to accountability for our waywardness in causing harm. Third, governments and other authorities have responsibility to implement equitable civil and criminal laws as a curb against human misbehavior. The Universal Declaration of Human Rights aspires toward the rule of international law to transcend the improprieties of the laws of nations.[6] Ethical codes for specific professions establish "commonly accepted practices" to which practitioners are expected to conform. Finally, God raises up prophets to speak courageously and boldly against abuses of power when other measures fall short—as they always do—given the propensity of human beings for sinning.

In spite of these checks and balances intended to limit human perversity, the effects of sin on our lives remain pervasive and palpable. The realities of sin—whether personal or structural—cry out to God for repentance, amendment of life, forgiveness, and reconciliation. For Christians, therefore, the ethical life is always exercised between the possibility of unforgivable sins and the universal command of Jesus to forgive.

Between Unforgivable Sin and Unconditional Forgiveness

The ethics of forgiveness are lived out for Christians between two sayings of Jesus. The *first* is Jesus's naming that there is such a thing as the unforgivable sin: "Whoever speaks a word against the Son of Man will be forgiven, but whoever speaks against the Holy Spirit will not be forgiven, either in this age or in the age to come" (Matt 12:32). There has been fervent discussion about which exact sin Jesus had in mind. The reality is that Christian people experience the weight of many sins as being unforgivable, particularly when I myself or those dear to me have been grievously offended.

The *second* saying of Jesus opens up a contrasting horizon of meaning: "Then Peter came and said to him, 'Lord, if another member of the church sins against me, how often should I forgive? As many as seven times?' Jesus said to him, 'Not seven times, but, I tell you, seventy-seven times'" (Matt 18:21–22). The force of Jesus's reply to Peter is that we are to be as infinitely forgiving as God in Christ has forgiven us. Jesus's words to his enemies from the cross also set for us this example: "Father, forgive them; for they do not know what they are doing" (Luke 23:34).

When we speak of *the ethics of forgiveness*, we are referring to the intentional and disciplined reflection that Christians undertake, together with a community, about the concrete choices we must make in our lives about whether to forgive other people. Such choices confront us every day—in relationship to those near to us (our families, friends, or fellow church members) and in relationship to those who are strangers (including perpetrators of criminal acts or enemies in distant lands). How are we to deliberate an ethics of forgiveness in relationship to offenses of every kind, including gross violations against life itself? Moreover, how are we to practice an ethics of forgiveness in relating to those who have violated us personally?

Regardless of what Jesus meant by the unforgivable sin against the Holy Spirit, every day people experience painful injuries to their dignity and person. These experiences lead us to conclude that certain sins deserve not to be forgiven. Someone you believed to be your trusted friend betrays you in your hour of need. A neighbor is identified as the source of vicious rumors that have tarnished your reputation. A member of your family is caught stealing from your bank account. A child is sexually violated by a parent. A member of your church is violently murdered by an intruder in her own home. Someone who is intoxicated swerves into the oncoming lane and kills innocent people. There are many sins committed against us or against others that we experience as deserving no forgiveness.

Some of these are hideous acts that destroy the precious gift of physical life: murder or genocide. Other acts, while sparing physical life, turn existence into a living hell: sexual abuse, rape, or torture. What can be done to restore a life that has been extinguished? What can be done to repair the traumatic memories of those who have been emotionally and physically desecrated?[7] Righteousness leads us to conclude that for these sins, no forgiveness is possible.

For Christians, the source and norm for all forgiveness is Jesus Christ. One of the most scandalous practices of Jesus was daring to forgive sins, especially the sins of notorious public sinners (cf. Luke 7:47–50). Jesus forgave people whom righteous ones claimed deserved condemnation (cf. Luke 18:9–14).

Nowhere is the challenge of forgiveness more incisive than in Jesus's command "Love your enemies and pray for those who persecute you" (Matt 5:44). Jesus taught his disciples the way of forgiveness in the Lord's Prayer: "Forgive us our sins, as we forgive those who sin against us" (Luke 11:4 NLT). Notice the connection between our receiving forgiveness and the expectation that we forgive the sins of others.

The cross of Jesus Christ reveals that the very heart of God is merciful and forgiving. Jesus's death on the cross, Christians confess, is for the sins of the world: "And when you were dead in trespasses and the uncircumcision of your flesh, God made you alive together with him, when he forgave us all our trespasses, erasing the record that stood against us with its legal demands. He set this aside, nailing it to the cross" (Col 2:13–14). Jesus Christ is "the Lamb of God who takes away the sin of the world" (John 1:29). Given the clarity of New Testament testimony to the power of the cross of Christ to forgive sins, we may imagine that the sin "against the Holy Spirit" could refer to those who contradict the truth that God has the power to forgive all sins!

Forgiveness as Process

Although the New Testament is abundantly clear that the cross of Jesus Christ is the ground of God's unconditional and complete forgiveness, our human capacity to forgive remains reluctant and limited. We long for the eschatological future wherein God will be all in all, when forgiveness will be real and reconciliation manifest (cf. 1 Cor 15:28). In the *mean* time, we often struggle with the meaning of Christ's forgiveness for our lives, especially when we feel that the other person is undeserving. In some cases—for example, those having suffered from sexual abuse—no expectations should be imposed on victims about the need to forgive. There are many situations, both in daily life and on the horizon of international relations, where it is easy to believe that forgiveness is not possible.

The ultimate goal of forgiving is to attain reconciliation. Several factors foster the possible movement from injury to forgiveness and reconciliation: contrition, repentance, acceptance of responsibility, reparations, healing, and reunion. In cases where the offender is ready to confess wrongdoing, repent, and make amends, the process of forgiveness leading to reconciliation is facilitated. Where someone admits fault and demonstrates true contrition, this process can result in profound gratitude and joy (cf. Luke 15:11–32).

In few circumstances, however, are all of these elements present, which provide the ideal conditions for forgiveness and reconciliation. The offender may not demonstrate genuine, or even minimal, contrition or repentance. There may be no acceptance of responsibility or willingness to make amends. The violation may be so extreme as to summon forth only feelings of rage and desire for revenge. In the most tragic instances, the victims may no longer be alive to engage in the ethics of forgiveness for themselves. How do the loved ones of those victimized by murder or genocide begin to engage in the process leading toward forgiveness and reconciliation? Forgiveness is facilitated under the conditions where the offender demonstrates remorse, repents, and makes amends. Forgiveness is complicated by the lack of these conditions.

By our own powers, many circumstances would prevent us from forgiving. In myriad ways, forgiveness is always a miracle granted by the power of God. Only because of what God has done in Jesus Christ can we dare to enter into the process leading toward forgiveness, especially when souls and bodies have suffered severe trauma. The ethics of forgiveness can entail a profound struggle. It may take many years of prayer, conversation with trusted friends, and counseling to reach the point of surrender, when the heart might be ready to forgive. In contexts of extreme violence, a process of truth and reconciliation may need to be conducted in order that some measure of justice is done for the victims, such as has been set forth in South Africa, Peru, or Rwanda. How might such a truth and reconciliation process provide a new framework for making reparations to Indigenous people and African American people in the US?[8]

It is for Christ's sake that Christians are summoned to enter into a process that can lead to forgiveness. Reinhold Niebuhr wrote,

> Nothing that is worth doing can be achieved in our lifetime; therefore we must be saved by hope. Nothing which is true or beautiful or good makes complete sense in any immediate context of history; therefore we must be saved by faith. Nothing we do, however virtuous, can be accomplished alone; therefore we must be saved by love. No virtuous act is quite as virtuous from the standpoint of our friend or foe as it is from our standpoint. Therefore we must be saved by the final form of love which is forgiveness.[9]

Ultimately, it is only because we have a merciful God who has forgiven all our sins that we dare to imagine loving our enemies and forgiving those who have violated us or our loved ones. As 1 John 4 says, "In this is love, not that we loved God but that he loved us and sent his Son to be the atoning sacrifice for our sins. . . . God is love, and those who abide in love abide in God, and God abides in them. . . . We love because [God] first loved us" (vv. 10, 16b, 19).

Christ Will Come Again to Judge the Living and the Dead

Where the ethics of forgiveness fails to lead to reconciliation between the offended and offenders, final consolation derives from the promise of God's eternity. The Christian church holds both that Christ will come again as judge of all and that the cross of Christ is the basis for eternal forgiveness. This means that God in Christ will deal righteously with all those who have committed sins against their neighbors, meting out perfect justice. However, this also means God in Christ will hold us accountable for how we have forgiven those who have sinned against us. How God finally arbitrates between the demands of justice and the revelation of complete forgiveness in Christ is one of the deepest mysteries of the faith. Forgiveness remains therefore a process in this world awaiting eschatological resolution.

We conclude this book with a biblical reference to what it means for us as human beings to be created in the image of God. In the ancient world, kings sometimes established their territory by setting up images of themselves to remind all those who would gaze upon their visage who was the ruler there. As often as one would look upon the image of the king, one was summoned to remember the sovereign to whom one was ultimately accountable in this land.[10]

For Lutheran ethics, the biblical teaching about human beings created in God's image (Gen 1:26) is a reminder that when we look at our neighbor, we are looking upon the image of God in that person, and we are reminded of the One to whom we are ultimately accountable. The Jewish philosopher Emmanuel Levinas proposed that the human face is the nearest revelation of God's presence in this world. To view the human face and encounter the human person is to know and pay respect to the One who created us in that image. Imagine an ethics that pays utmost respect to the inherent dignity to each one created in God's image. Jesus Christ came to restore among us the image of the invisible God (Col 1:15). Lutheran ethics is finally neighbor ethics. The gospel of Jesus Christ sets us free to serve neighbors and their well-being. Only that!

Notes

Introduction

1 Cf. Lawrence Kohlberg, *The Philosophy of Moral Development: Moral Stages and the Idea of Justice*, vol. 1, *Essays on Moral Development* (New York: Harper & Row, 1981).

2 Dietrich Bonhoeffer, *Ethics*, ed. Clifford J. Green, trans. Reinhard Krauss, Charles C. West, and Douglas W. Stott, Dietrich Bonhoeffer Works 6 (Minneapolis: Fortress, 2005), 49.

3 This text focuses on the usable contributions of Luther for ethics today. Elsewhere, I have analyzed and criticized the disastrous failures of Luther in relation to his engagement with the Anabaptists, the Peasants' Revolt, and the Jews. I call on congregations and educational institutions to teach with historical honesty about these cases and to repudiate Luther's writings against the Jews. See Craig L. Nessan, "Beyond Luther to Ethical Reformation: Peasants, Anabaptists, Jews," in *Radicalizing Reformation: North American Perspectives*, ed. Karen L. Bloomquist, Craig L. Nessan, and Hans G. Ulrich (Berlin: Lit Verlag, 2016), 6:151–78.

4 Martin Luther, "How Christians Should Regard Moses," in *The Annotated Luther: Word and Faith*, ed. Kirsi I. Stjerna (Minneapolis Fortress, 2015), 2:143–49.

5 Saint Aurelius Augustine, "#110: Augustine's Love Sermon," Christian History Institute, accessed June 29, 2021, https://christianhistoryinstitute.org/study/module/augustine.

6   For example, Joseph Fletcher, *Situation Ethics: The New Morality* (Louisville, KY: Westminster John Knox, 1997).

7   Alasdair MacIntyre, *After Virtue: A Study in Moral Theory* (Notre Dame, IN: University of Notre Dame Press, 2007). Cf. Joel D. Biermann, *A Case for Character: Towards a Lutheran Virtue Ethics* (Minneapolis: Fortress, 2014).

8   Friedrich Daniel Ernst Schleiermacher, *Christian Faith: A New Translation and Critical Edition*, ed. and trans. Terrence N. Tice, Catherine L. Kelsey, and Edwina Lawler (Louisville, KY: Westminster John Knox, 2016); Friedrich Daniel Ernst Schleiermacher, *Selections from Friedrich Schleiermacher's Christian Ethics*, ed. and trans. James M. Brandt (Louisville, KY: Westminster John Knox, 2010); Johann Christian Konrad von Hofmann, *Der Schriftbeweis: Ein theologischer Versuch*, 2 vols. (Nördlingen, Germany: C. H. Beck, 1857–60); Johann Christian Konrad von Hofmann, *Theologische Ethik* (Nördlingen, Germany: C. H. Beck, 1878); Friedrich Bauer et al., *Christliche Dogmatik auf lutherische Grundlage* (Neuendettelsau, Germany: Missionsanstalt, 1921); Friedrich Bauer et al., *Christliche Ethik auf lutherische Grundlage* (Neuendettelsau, Germany: Missionsanstalt, 1904).

9   Paul Althaus, *Die Christliche Wahrheit. Lehrbuch der Dogmatik*, 8th ed. (Gütersloh, Germany: Gütersloher Verlag, 1969); Paul Althaus, *Grundriß der Ethik* (Erlangen, Germany: R. Merkel, 1931); Werner Elert, *Der Christliche Glaube: Grundlinien der Lutherischen Dogmatik* (Berlin: Furche Verlag, 1960); Werner Elert, *The Structure of Lutheranism*, trans. Walter A. Hansen (St. Louis, MO: Concordia, 1962); Werner Elert, *The Christian Ethos: The Foundations of the Christian Way of Life*, trans. Carl J. Schindler (Philadelphia: Fortress, 1957); Helmut Thielicke, *The Christian Faith*, ed. and trans. Geoffrey W. Bromiley, 3 vols. (Grand Rapids, MI: Eerdmans, 1974–82); Helmut Thielicke, *Theological Ethics*, vol. 1, *Foundations*, ed. and trans. William H. Lazareth (Philadelphia: Fortress, 1966); Helmut Thielicke, *Theological Ethics*, vol. 2, *Politics*, ed. and trans. William H. Lazareth (Philadelphia: Fortress, 1969).

10 Bonhoeffer, *Ethics*.

11 George Wolfgang Forell, *Faith Active in Love: An Investigation of the Principles Underlying Luther's Social Ethics* (New York: American Press, 1954); Karen L. Bloomquist and John R. Stumme, eds., *The Promise of Lutheran Ethics* (Minneapolis: Fortress, 1998); William H. Lazareth, *Christians in Society: Luther, the Bible, and Social Ethics* (Minneapolis: Fortress, 2001); Oswald Bayer, *Freedom in Response: Lutheran Ethics: Sources and Controversies*, trans. Jeffrey Cayzer (New York: Oxford University Press, 2007); Walter Altmann, *Luther and Liberation: A Latin American Perspective*, 2nd ed. (Minneapolis: Fortress, 2015).

12 Paul Ricoeur, *Interpretation Theory: Discourse and the Surplus of Meaning* (Fort Worth: Texas Christian University Press, 1976).

13 Paul Ricoeur, *The Conflict of Interpretations: Essays in Hermeneutics*, ed. Don Ihde (Evanston, IL: Northwestern University Press, 1974).

Chapter One

1 Cf. Robin Parry, "Reader-Response Criticism," in *Dictionary for Theological Interpretation of the Bible*, ed. Kevin J. Vanhoozer (Grand Rapids, MI: Baker Academic, 2005), 658–61.

2 Cf. A. K. M. Adam, *What Is Postmodern Biblical Criticism?* (Minneapolis: Fortress, 1995), 27–30.

3 Note the important distinction between "literalism," which is used to refer to verbal inspiration and propositional revelation as represented in fundamentalism, and "literal sense," which describes Luther's approach to Scripture.

4 Developed in the nineteenth century, "dispensationalism" is an approach to interpreting Christian history as the unfolding of predetermined stages based on God's plan revealed in the Bible; cf. Mitri Raheb, *Faith in the Face of Empire: The Bible through Palestinian Eyes* (Maryknoll, NY: Orbis, 2014).

5 Yves M. J. Congar, *I Believe in the Holy Spirit*, trans. David Smith (New York: Seabury, 1983), 3:271.

6 Regin Prenter, *Spiritus Creator: Luther's Concept of the Holy Spirit*, trans. John M. Jensen (Philadelphia: Muhlenberg, 1953), 102.

7 Prenter, 129–30.

8 Paul Althaus, *The Theology of Martin Luther*, trans. Robert C. Schultz (Philadelphia: Fortress, 1966), 391–99.

9 George Wolfgang Forell, "Why Recall Luther Today," *Word & World* 3, no. 4 (1983): 341.

10 Willem Jan Kooiman, *Luther and the Bible*, trans. John Schmidt (Philadelphia: Muhlenberg, 1961), 227–28.

11 Kooiman, 237.

12 Martin Luther, *Luthers Werke, Weimar Ausgabe* 16:82, as quoted in Kooiman, *Luther and the Bible*, 237–38.

13 Martin Luther, "How Christians Should Regard Moses," in *Luther's Works*, ed. E. Theodore Bachman (Philadelphia: Fortress, 1960), 35:170 (hereafter cited as LW 35).

14 Bernhard Lohse, *Martin Luther's Theology: Its Historical and Systematic Development*, trans. and ed. Roy A. Harrisville (Minneapolis: Fortress, 1999), 190.

15 Cf. Robert W. Jenson, "Luther's Contemporary Theological Significance," in *The Cambridge Companion to Martin Luther*, ed. Donald K. McKim (Cambridge: Cambridge University Press, 2003), 284–86.

16 Althaus, *Theology of Martin Luther*, 76–78.

17 Cf. Rudolf Bultmann, "Is Exegesis without Presuppositions Possible?," in *Existence and Faith*, trans. Schubert M. Ogden (New York: Meridian, 1960), 289–96.

18 Martin Luther, "Preface to the Old Testament," in LW 35:236.

19 Werner Elert, *Law and Gospel*, trans. Edward H. Schroeder (Philadelphia: Fortress, 1967), 7–13.

20 Oswald Bayer, "Luther as an Interpreter of Holy Scripture," in McKim, *Cambridge Companion*, 75–77.

21 Ritva H. Williams, *The Bible's Importance for the Church Today* (Minneapolis: Augsburg Fortress, 2009), 49.

22 Prenter, *Spiritus Creator*, 115.

23 Williams, *Bible's Importance*, 50.

24 Regarding Luther's deliberation of the value of these books, see Kooiman, *Luther and the Bible*, 110–16.

25 Cf. Ernst Käsemann, "The Canon of the New Testament and the Unity of the Church," in *Essays on New Testament Themes*, trans. W. J. Montague (London: SCM, 1964), 95–107.

26 In the history of the contemporary ecumenical movement, we are witnessing the growing recognition that denominational differences in the interpretation of Scripture are complementary and not contradictory.

27 Eric W. Gritsch and Robert W. Jenson, *Lutheranism: The Theological Movement and Its Confessional Writings* (Philadelphia: Fortress, 1976), 6.

28 Dietrich Bonhoeffer, "Ultimate and Penultimate Things," in *Ethics*, 6:146–70.

29 Cf. Martin Luther, "How Christians Should Regard Moses," in LW 35:161–74, for his criteria in interpreting the law of Moses.

30 Martin Luther, "Last Sermon in Wittenberg" (second Sunday of Epiphany, January 17, 1546), in *Luthers Werke, Weimar Ausgabe* 51:126.

31 Richard Dawkins, *The God Delusion* (New York: Houghton Mifflin Harcourt, 2006), 221.

32 Cf. Hans-Georg Gadamer, *Truth and Method* (New York: Seabury, 1975).

33 Anthony C. Thiselton, "Hermeneutical Circle," in Vanhoozer, *Dictionary for Theological Interpretation*, 281–82.

34 Cf. Gerhard O. Forde, *Theology Is for Proclamation* (Minneapolis: Augsburg Fortress, 1990).

35 It is a hermeneutical "circle" insofar as the process of interpretation continues with ever-new readings of the text for ever-new contexts.

36 Cf. James Barr, *Fundamentalism* (Eugene, OR: Wipf & Stock, 2018), 160–86.

37 "Confession of Faith," chap. 2 in *Constitution, Bylaws, and Continuing Resolutions* (Chicago: Evangelical Lutheran Church in America, 2020), 2.02c.,

http://download.elca.org/ELCA%20Resource%20Repository/Constitutions
_Bylaws_and_Continuing_Resolutions_of_the_ELCA.pdf.

Chapter Two

1 The coining of the term is attributed to Albert C. Outler, ed., *John Wesley* (Oxford: Oxford University Press, 1970), iv. See also Don Thorson, *The Wesleyan Quadrilateral: Scripture, Tradition, Reason, and Experience as a Model of Evangelical Theology* (Lexington, KY: Emeth, 2005).

2 Ricoeur, *Interpretation Theory*.

3 On the significance of the term *classic*, see David Tracy, *The Analogical Imagination: Christian Theology and the Culture of Pluralism* (New York: Crossroad, 1981), 99–338.

4 Cf. George A. Lindbeck, *The Nature of Doctrine: Religion and Theology in a Postliberal Age* (Louisville, KY: Westminster John Knox, 1984), 32–37.

5 Cf. Ricoeur, *Conflict of Interpretations*.

6 Lutherans might well consider the justice trajectory as an exposition of the first use of the law in Lutheran categories.

7 Cf. Craig L. Nessan, *Many Members, Yet One Body: Committed Same-Gender Relationships and the Mission of the Church* (Minneapolis: Augsburg Fortress, 2004), 23–37.

8 See Jean-Francois Lyotard, *The Postmodern Condition: A Report on Knowledge*, trans. Geoff Bennington and Brian Massumi, with a foreword by Fredric Jameson (Minneapolis: University of Minnesota Press, 1984).

9 Cf. the classic treatment by Peter L. Berger and Thomas Luckmann, *The Social Construction of Reality: A Treatise on the Sociology of Knowledge* (New York: Anchor, 1966).

10 Cf. Jennifer Baldwin, ed., *Navigating Post-Truth and Alternative Facts: Religion and Science as Political Theology* (Lanham, MD: Lexington Books, 2018).

11 David Tracy, *Fragments: The Existential Situation of Our Time, Selected Essays* (Chicago: University of Chicago Press, 2020), 1:278.

12 Robert John Russell, "Ian Barbour's Methodology in Science and Religion," Dialogue: Theology and Science, accessed February 10, 2020, https://www.theologie-naturwissenschaften.de/en/dialogue-between-theology-and-science/editorials/barboursmethodology/.

13 Cf. the methodology of S. Mark Heim, *Salvations: Truth and Difference in Religion* (Maryknoll, NY: Orbis, 1995), 215–29.

14 Pope Francis, *Fratelli tutti: Encyclical Letter of the Holy Father Francis on Fraternity and Social Friendship* (Rome: Vatican, 2020), para. 21, http://www.vatican.va/content/francesco/en/encyclicals/documents/papa-francesco_20201003_enciclica-fratelli-tutti.html.

15 "The Blind Men and the Elephant," Peace Corps, accessed June 29, 2021, https://www.peacecorps.gov/educators/resources/story-blind-men-and -elephant/.

Chapter Three

1 See the now classic treatment of Robert N. Bellah et al., *Habits of the Heart, with a New Preface: Individualism and Commitment in American Life* (Berkeley: University of California Press, 2007).

2 "First Amendment," Bill of Rights, Legal Information Institute, accessed August 6, 2020, https://www.law.cornell.edu/constitution/first_amendment.

3 Cf. Jacqueline A. Bussie, *Love without Limits: Jesus' Radical Vision for Love with No Exceptions* (Minneapolis: Fortress, 2018), 167–70.

4 Cf. Catherine Keller, *Political Theology of the Earth: Our Planetary Emergency and the Struggle for a New Public* (New York: Columbia University Press, 2018), 63–68.

5 Cf. Cynthia D. Moe-Lobeda, *Resisting Structural Evil: Love as Ecological-Economic Vocation* (Minneapolis: Fortress, 2013), 32–35.

6 Cf. William E. Connolly, *Capitalism and Christianity, American Style* (Durham, NC: Duke University Press, 2008), 39–67, on what Connolly, in chapter 2, calls "the evangelical-capitalist resonance machine."

7 See William T. Cavanaugh, *Field Hospital: The Church's Engagement with a Wounded World* (Grand Rapids, MI: Eerdmans, 2016), 23–31.

8 For a constructive approach to addressing global poverty, see Abhijit V. Banerjee and Esther Duflo, *Poor Economics: A Radical Rethinking of the Way to Fight Global Poverty* (New York: PublicAffairs, 2011).

9 See Martin Luther King Jr., *The Radical King* (Boston: Beacon, 2015), 87–91, for his critique of war in relation to poverty and racial injustice.

10 See Michelle Alexander, *The New Jim Crow: Mass Incarceration in the Age of Colorblindness* (New York: New Press, 2010).

11 For example, Philip Gorski, *American Covenant: A History of Civil Religion from the Puritans to the Present* (Princeton, NJ: Princeton University Press, 2017).

12 David Foster Wallace, *Infinite Jest* (New York: Little, Brown, 2006).

13 For example, Robert K. Bolger and Scott Korb, eds., *Gesturing toward Reality: David Foster Wallace and Philosophy* (New York: Bloomsbury, 2014).

14 David Foster Wallace, *This Is Water: Some Thoughts, Delivered on a Significant Occasion, about Living a Compassionate Life* (New York: Little, Brown, 2009). This is also available as David Foster Wallace, "This Is Water—Full Version—David Foster Wallace Commencement Speech," Lynn Skittle, May 19, 2013, YouTube video, 22:43, https://www.youtube.com/watch?v=8CrOL-ydFMI.

15 Wallace, *This Is Water*, 12, 14.

16 Wallace, 33.

17 Wallace, 36–37.

18 Wallace, 38, 44.

19 Wallace, 53.

20 Wallace, 60.

21 Wallace, 71, 85.

22 Wallace, 89.

23 Wallace, 96, 102.

24 Wallace, 106.

25 Wallace, 109.

26 Wallace, 110.

27 Wallace, 117.

28 Wallace, 120–21.

29 Wallace, 135.

30 "Confession and Forgiveness," in *Evangelical Lutheran Worship* (Minneapolis: Augsburg Fortress, 2006), 95.

31 *The Small Catechism of Martin Luther*, "The Ten Commandments," "Meaning of the Eighth Commandment," in *Evangelical Lutheran Worship*, 1161.

32 Cf. Ernst Käsemann, *Jesus Means Freedom* (Philadelphia: Fortress, 1969).

33 C. F. W. Walther, *The Proper Distinction between Law and Gospel*, trans. W. H. T. Dahl (St. Louis, MO: Concordia, 1986).

34 There are also theological grounds for defending three uses of the law, the third interpreting the law as a guide for the Christian life. See chapter 5 for further discussion of the uses of the law.

35 Cf. J. L. Austin, *How to Do Things with Words* (Cambridge, MA: Harvard University Press, 1962), 4–11.

36 See Norma Cook Everist, *Seventy Images of Grace in the Epistles* (Eugene, OR: Wipf & Stock, 2015).

37 Martin Luther, *The Freedom of a Christian*, in *The Annotated Luther: The Roots of Reform*, ed. Timothy J. Wengert (Minneapolis: Fortress, 2015), 1:488.

38 Luther, 1:500.

39 Bayer, *Freedom in Response*, 86, refers to this as the "joyous exchange."

40 Luther, *Freedom of a Christian*, 1:520.

41 Cf. Craig L. Nessan, *Shalom Church: The Body of Christ as Ministering Community* (Minneapolis: Fortress, 2010), 126–27.

42 Cf. the perspectives from other Christian traditions in Al Truesdale, ed., *All Things Needed for Godliness: A Portrait of Holiness among Christian Traditions* (Kansas City, MO: Foundry, 2020).

43 See Lazareth, *Christians in Society*, 221, who cites from the conclusion of Luther's *The Freedom of a Christian*: "I will do nothing in this life, except what I see is necessary, profitable, and salutary to my neighbor, since through faith I have an abundance of good things in Christ."

44 Foster Wallace did express an intuition that religious power was useful for transcending the "default setting." See Wallace, *This Is Water*, 102. Nevertheless, he did not sufficiently develop the implications of this insight.

Chapter Four

1 For an introduction to some of the critical problems, cf. W. D. J. Cargill Thompson, *The Political Thought of Martin Luther* (Totowa, NJ: Barnes & Noble, 1984), 36–37.

2 See Nessan, "Beyond Luther," 6:151–78.

3 Reinhold Seeberg, *Christliche Ethik* (Stuttgart: W. Kohlhammer, 1936), 65–66.

4 Seeberg, 231–32, 266–69.

5 Altmann, *Luther and Liberation*, 180–99.

6 Cf. Craig L. Nessan, "Liberation Theologies Critique of Luther's Two Kingdoms Doctrine," *Currents in Theology and Mission* 16 (August 1989): 257–66.

7 Cf. Ulrich Duchrow, Wolfgang Huber, and Louis Reith, eds., *Umdeutungen der Zweireichelehre Luthers im 19. Jahrhundert: Texte zur Kirchen- und Theologiegeschichte* (Gütersloh, Germany: Gerd Mohn, 1976).

8 A summary of Duchrow's argument is found in Karl H. Hertz, ed., *Two Kingdoms and One World: A Sourcebook in Christian Ethics* (Minneapolis: Augsburg, 1976), 70–75.

9 Ulrich Duchrow, *Global Economy: A Confessional Issue for the Churches?*, trans. David Lewis (Geneva: WCC, 1987), 9–15.

10 Hertz, *Two Kingdoms*, 157. Vitor Westhelle points out that the two kingdoms teaching first was named a "doctrine" in the essays of Franz Lau in 1933 and Harald Diem in 1938. Cf. Vitor Westhelle, "God and Justice: The Word and the Mask," *Journal of Lutheran Ethics* 3, no. 1 (January 2003): para. 3, https://elca.org/JLE/Articles/895.

11 Karl Barth offered early and strenuous criticism. Cf. Eric W. Gritsch, *Martin—God's Court Jester: Luther in Retrospect* (Philadelphia: Fortress, 1983), 112.

12 Cf. Westhelle, "God and Justice," paras. 24–28.

13 On the origins of disestablishment of religion, see Martin E. Marty, *Righteous Empire: The Protestant Experience in America* (New York: Dial, 1970), 35–45.

14 Cf. the analysis of Sidney E. Mead, *The Lively Experiment: The Shaping of Christianity in America* (New York: Harper & Row, 1963), 134–42.

15 Cf. Altmann, *Luther and Liberation*, 182–84.

16 Bruce Chilton, *Pure Kingdom: Jesus' Vision of God* (Grand Rapids, MI: Eerdmans, 1996), 23–44.

17 Cf. the analysis and conclusions of Norman Perrin, *Jesus and the Language of the Kingdom: Symbol and Metaphor in New Testament Interpretation* (Philadelphia: Fortress, 1976), 40–56, 194–204.

18 Cf. Thompson, *Political Thought*, 38–39, 53–56.

19 See Heiko A. Oberman, *Luther: Man between God and the Devil*, trans. Eileen Walliser-Schwarzbart (New Haven, CT: Yale University Press, 1989). Cf. also the model of Ulrich Duchrow, ed., *Lutheran Churches—Salt or Mirror of Society* (Geneva: Lutheran World Federation, 1977), 6–7.

20 Cf. the discussion of the battle between God and Satan in Gustaf Wingren, *Luther on Vocation*, trans. Carl C. Rasmussen (Philadelphia: Muhlenberg, 1957), 23–37.

21 Cf. the bibliography informing the discussion of these distinctions in Gerhard Sauter, ed., *Zur Zwei-Reiche-Lehre Luthers* (Munich: Chr. Kaiser, 1973), 225–27, especially the references to Wilfred Joest and Hans-Jürgen Schrey.

22 Cf. the discussion of the problems and proper interpretation of Luther's Zwei-Reiche-Lehre and Zwei-Regimente-Lehre in Thompson, *Political Thought*, 36–61.

23 This is a constructive contemporary translation of the German word *Regimente*.

24 Cf. Thompson, *Political Thought*, 43–44.

25 Cf. Luther, *Freedom of a Christian*, 1:487–538.

26 Cf. Mary Solberg, *Compelling Knowledge: A Feminist Proposal for an Epistemology of the Cross* (Albany: State University of New York Press, 1997).

27 Gary M. Simpson, "Toward a Lutheran 'Delight in the Law of the Lord': Church and State in the Context of Civil Society," in *Church and State: Lutheran Perspectives*, ed. John R. Stumme and Robert W. Tuttle (Minneapolis: Fortress, 2003), 32–33.

28 While God places all human beings in stations, Christians are called to live out those stations according to their baptismal identity. Cf. Wingren, *Luther on Vocation*, 4–10.

29 See Susan Kosche Vallem, "Promoting the General Welfare: Lutheran Social Ministry," in Stumme and Tuttle, *Church and State*, 88–91.

30 Gustaf Wingren, *Creation and Law*, trans. Ross MacKenzie (Philadelphia: Muhlenberg, 1961), 48–49.

31 Cf. Lohse, *Martin Luther's Theology*, 267–73.

32 On the work of evangelizing, see chapter 7 in Richard H. Bliese and Craig Van Gelder, eds., *The Evangelizing Church: A Lutheran Contribution* (Minneapolis: Fortress, 2005), 113–32.

33 Cf. Lohse, *Martin Luther's Theology*, 258–66.

34 Cf. Nessan, *Shalom Church*, chap. 1.

Chapter Five

1 The classic treatment is Prenter, *Spiritus Creator*.

2 Martin Luther, "The Third Article: On Being Made Holy," *The Small Catechism*, in *The Book of Concord: The Confessions of the Evangelical Lutheran Church*, ed. Robert Kolb and Timothy J. Wengert (Minneapolis: Fortress, 2000), 355–56.

3 Cf. Martin Luther, "The Second Article: On Redemption," *The Small Catechism*, in Kolb and Wengert, *Book of Concord*, 355.

4 "The Augsburg Confession," in Kolb and Wengert, *Book of Concord*, 41, art. 4, "Concerning Justification."

5 Martin Luther, *The Smalcald Articles*, in Kolb and Wengert, *Book of Concord*, 301, pt. 2, art. 1.

6 For example, Carl E. Braaten, *Justification: The Article by which the Church Stands or Falls* (Minneapolis: Fortress, 1990).

7 Gerhard Forde, "The Lutheran View," in *Christian Spirituality: Five Views of Sanctification*, ed. Donald L. Alexander (Downers Grove, IL: InterVarsity, 1988), 13.

8 Dietrich Bonhoeffer, *Discipleship*, ed. Geffrey B. Kelly and John D. Godsey, trans. Barbara Green and Reinhard Krauss (Minneapolis: Fortress, 2001), 53.

9 Martin Luther, *The Freedom of a Christian*, in LW 31:344.

10 Luther, 31:346, 351.

11 Luther, 31:365.

12 Martin Luther, *Two Kinds of Righteousness*, in LW 31:297, 299.

13 Philip Melanchthon, *Loci Communes* (1543), trans. J. A. O. Preus (St. Louis, MO: Concordia, 1992), 74, "The Use of the Law."

14 For example, Scott R. Murray, *Law, Life, and the Living God: The Third Use of Law in Modern American Lutheranism* (St. Louis, MO: Concordia, 2002).

15 *Formula of Concord*, in Kolb and Wengert, *Book of Concord*, 502, art. 6.1, "Concerning the Third Use of the Law."

16 *Formula of Concord*, 503, art. 6, "Negative Theses: False and Contrary Teaching."

17 *Formula of Concord*, 503, art. 6.6, "Concerning the Third Use of the Law."

18 Heinrich Schmid, *The Doctrinal Theology of the Evangelical Lutheran Church: Verified from the Original Sources*, trans. Charles A. Hay and Henry E. Jacobs, 4th ed. (Philadelphia: Lutheran Publication Society, 1899), 424–41.

19 Schmid, 441–91.

20 Schmid, 486–87.

21 Schmid, 491–99.

22 Schmid, 491–92.

23 Philipp Jakob Spener, *Pia Desideria*, trans. Theodore G. Tappert (Philadelphia: Fortress, 1964).

24 Summarized from Douglas H. Shantz, *An Introduction to German Pietism: Protestant Renewal at the Dawn of Modern Europe*, with a foreword by Peter C. Erb (Baltimore: Johns Hopkins University Press, 2013), 89–91.

25 Shantz, 284.

26 *Following Our Shepherd to Full Communion: Report of the Lutheran–Moravian Dialogue with Recommendations for Full Communion in Worship, Fellowship, and Mission* (Chicago: Evangelical Lutheran Church in America, 1998), 30.

27 *Following Our Shepherd*, 28, 31.

28 Murray, *Law, Life, and the Living God*, 217.

29 Lazareth, *Christians in Society*, 199, 205.

30 Lazareth, 224.

31 Lazareth, 234.

32 Bonhoeffer, *Discipleship*, 259.

33 Bonhoeffer, 259.

34 Cf. James L. Bailey, *Contrast Community: Practicing the Sermon on the Mount* (Eugene, OR: Wipf & Stock, 2013).

35 Bonhoeffer, *Discipleship*, 261.

36 Bonhoeffer, 276.

37 Tuomo Mannermaa, *Christ Present in Faith: Luther's View of Justification*, ed. Kirsi Stjerna (Minneapolis: Fortress, 2005), 49 (italics removed).

38 Mannermaa, 84, 85–86.

39 Mannermaa, 87–88. Mannermaa introduces the Orthodox understanding of "divinization" to characterize Luther's position, a theme not taken up in this chapter. See also Tuomo Mannermaa, *Two Kinds of Love: Martin Luther's Religious World*, trans. and ed. Kirsi I. Stjerna (Minneapolis: Fortress, 2010).

40 In the Affirmation of Baptism rite, the baptized promise "to live among God's faithful people, to hear the word of God and share in the Lord's Supper, to proclaim the good news of God in Christ through word and deed, to serve all people, following the example of Jesus, and to strive for justice and peace in all the earth." *Evangelical Lutheran Worship*, 236.

41 Wingren, *Luther on Vocation*.

Chapter Six

1   Cf. Mark Tranvik, *Martin Luther and the Called Life* (Minneapolis: Fortress, 2016), 164.

2   Luther, *Smalcald Articles*, 301 (pt. 2, art. 5). Cf. also Martin Luther, *Selected Psalms III*, in LW 14:37.

3   Lutheran World Federation and the Roman Catholic Church, *Joint Declaration on the Doctrine of Justification* (Grand Rapids, MI: Eerdmans, 2000).

4   Jürgen Moltmann, "Reformation and Revolution," in *Martin Luther and the Modern Mind*, ed. Manfred Hoffmann, Toronto Studies in Theology 22 (Lewiston, NY: Edwin Mellon, 1985), 86, cited in Kathryn Kleinhans, "The Work of a Christian: Vocation in Lutheran Perspective," *Word & World* 25 (Fall 2005): 395.

5   Martin Luther, *To the Christian Nobility of the German People* (1520), trans. Charles M. Jacobs, in LW 44:127.

6   Luther, 44:128.

7   Cf. Timothy J. Wengert, *Priesthood, Pastors, Bishops: Public Ministry for the Reformation and Today* (Minneapolis: Fortress, 2008), 7–8.

8   Nathan Montover, *Luther's Revolution: The Political Dimensions of Martin Luther's Universal Priesthood* (Cambridge: James Clarke, 2011), 56.

9   Martin Luther, "Commentary on Psalm 110," in LW 13:330–31, as cited in Montover, *Luther's Revolution*, 62.

10   Martin Luther, "Sermon at the Dedication of Castle Church, Torgau," in LW 51:335, as cited in Montover, *Luther's Revolution*, 63.

11   Montover, *Luther's Revolution*, 64–65.

12   Martin Luther, *The Freedom of a Christian* (1520), trans. Mark D. Tranvik (Minneapolis: Fortress, 2008), 50.

13   Luther, 84.

14   Craig L. Nessan, "Law, Righteousness, Reason, Will, and Works: Civil and Theological Uses," *Currents in Theology and Mission* 41 (February 2014): 55–56.

15   Luther, *Freedom of a Christian*, 88.

16   Wengert, *Priesthood, Pastors, Bishops*, 5; cf. Wengert, 7–14. The German word *Amt* here will be translated as "arena," not "office."

17   Martin Luther, *On the Councils and the Church* (1539), trans. Charles M. Jacobs and Eric W. Gritsch, in LW 41:177. The word government(s) here is rendered as "arena(s)."

18   Cf. Wingren, *Luther on Vocation*, 140, on the "masks" of God. This point deserves far greater elaboration, insofar as it locates vocation within God's good creation with significance for all people. Cf. Kathryn A. Kleinhans, "Places of Responsibility: Educating for Multiple Callings in Multiple Communities," in *At This Time and in This Place: Vocation and Higher*

Education, ed. David S. Cunningham (New York: Oxford University Press, 2015).

19 Cf. Risto Saarinen, "Ethics in Luther's Theology: The Three Orders," in *Moral Philosophy on the Threshold of Modernity*, ed. Jill Kraye and Risto Saarinen, The New Synthese Historical Library 57 (Dordrecht: Springer, 2005). Whereas Luther employed different expressions, including order (Ordnung, *ordo, ordinatio*), hierarchy (*hierarchia*), establishment (Stifft), right (Recht), estate (Stand), order of life or life-form (*genus vitae*), I will use the term *arena* to name this feature of Luther's theology.

20 Wingren, *Luther on Vocation*, 27.

21 Kleinhans, "Places of Responsibility," 107.

22 Luther, *Christian Nobility*, 44:130; Wengert, *Priesthood, Pastors, Bishops*, 13.

23 Cf. Philip Jenkins, *The New Faces of Christianity: Believing the Bible in the Global South* (New York: Oxford University Press, 2006).

24 "Affirmation of Baptism," in *Evangelical Lutheran Worship*, 237.

25 Martin Luther, *The Babylonian Captivity of the Church* (1520), trans. A. T. W. Steinhäuser, in LW 36:112–13.

26 Craig L. Nessan, "The Neighborliness (*Diakonia*) of All Believers: Toward Reimagining the Universal Priesthood," in *Together by Grace: Introducing the Lutherans*, ed. Kathryn A. Kleinhans (Minneapolis: Augsburg Fortress, 2016), 143–46.

27 For a theological elaboration on the meaning, convictions, and disciplines of neighborliness, see Peter Block, Walter Brueggemann, and John McKnight, *An Other Kingdom: Departing the Consumer Culture* (Hoboken, NJ: John Wiley & Sons, 2016), especially chapters 2 and 6.

28 For a primer on the significance of liturgical worship, see Gordon W. Lathrop, *Central Things: Worship in Word and Sacrament* (Minneapolis: Augsburg Fortress, 2005).

29 Martin Luther, *The Blessed Sacrament of the Holy and True Body of Christ, and the Brotherhoods* (1519), in LW 35:67.

30 For the following, see Nessan, *Shalom Church*.

31 Two classic treatments are Jürgen Moltmann, *The Crucified God: The Cross of Christ as the Foundation and Criticism of Christian Theology*, trans. R. A. Wilson and John Bowden (Minneapolis: Fortress, 1993); and Douglas John Hall, *Lighten Our Darkness: Toward an Indigenous Theology of the Cross* (Louisville, KY: Westminster John Knox, 1976).

32 Martin Luther, "Prefaces to the New Testament," in LW 35:370–71.

33 Charles Taylor, *Sources of the Self* (Cambridge: Cambridge University Press, 1989), 218.

34 "About the Initiative," Life of Faith Initiative, accessed September 9, 2020, http://lifeoffaith.info/.

35 "Our Vision," Life of Faith Initiative, accessed June 29, 2021, https://lifeoffaith.info/about/our-vision/.

36 John Rawls, *A Theory of Justice* (Cambridge, MA: Belknap, 1971), employs the term *leximin* (the law of attending to the marginalized) as fundamental principle of a just society.

Chapter Seven

1 Martin Luther, "The Heidelberg Disputation," in Wengert, *Annotated Luther*, 1:84.

2 Cf. Dietrich Bonhoeffer, "The View from Below," in *Letters and Papers from Prison*, ed. Eberhard Bethge, trans. Reginald Fuller and John Bowden (New York: Touchstone, 1997), 17.

3 Søren Kierkegaard, *The Sickness unto Death: A Christian Psychological Exposition for Upbuilding and Awakening*, ed. and trans. Howard V. Hong and Edna H. Hong (Princeton, NJ: Princeton University Press, 1983).

4 Elaine Scarry, *The Body in Pain: The Making and Unmaking of a World* (New York: Oxford University Press, 1985), 54.

5 Cf. Duane Larson and Jeff Zust, *Care for the Sorrowing Soul: Healing Moral Injuries from Military Service and Implications for the Rest of Us* (Eugene, OR: Wipf & Stock, 2017).

6 See Moe-Lobeda, *Resisting Structural Evil*.

7 See Ernst Bloch, *The Spirit of Utopia*, trans. Anthony A. Nassar (Stanford: Stanford University Press, 2000).

8 See "Universal Declaration of Human Rights," United Nations, accessed June 29, 2021, https://www.un.org/en/about-us/universal-declaration-of-human-rights.

9 Social statements can serve as study materials for the church as a teaching and learning community to engage and respond to urgent issues facing our society and world. The social statements of the Evangelical Lutheran Church in America provide examples of the range of available topics: "Social Statements," Evangelical Lutheran Church in America, accessed June 29, 2021, https://elca.org/Faith/Faith-and-Society/Social-Statements.

10 Martin Luther, *Letters 1*, in LW 48:281–82.

11 For a profound exploration of the theological significance of the cross and the silence of Jesus's death, see Alan E. Lewis, *Between Cross and Resurrection: A Theology of Holy Saturday* (Grand Rapids, MI: Eerdmans, 2001).

12 See Jon Sobrino, *Where Is God? Earthquake, Terrorism, Barbarity, and Hope*, trans. Margaret Wilde (Maryknoll, NY: Orbis, 2004), who references the experiences of "crucified people" yet today.

13 Theologically and ethically, it is far more compelling to confess the alternative rendering: "He descended into hell."

14 Jürgen Moltmann, *The Spirit of Hope: Theology for a World in Peril* (Louisville, KY: Westminster John Knox, 2019), 170.

15 Luther, "Heidelberg Disputation," 1:83–84.

16 Cf. Lohse, *Martin Luther's Theology*, 39.

17 These include Jürgen Moltmann, *The Crucified God*, trans. R. A. Wilson and John Bowden (New York: Harper & Row, 1974); Hall, *Lighten Our Darkness*; Alister E. McGrath, *Luther's Theology of the Cross: Martin Luther's Theological Breakthrough* (Oxford: Blackwell, 1985); Charles B. Cousar, *The Theology of the Cross: The Death of Jesus in the Pauline Letters* (Minneapolis: Augsburg Fortress, 1990); Winston D. Persaud, *The Theology of the Cross and Marx's Anthropology: A View from the Caribbean* (New York: Peter Lang, 1991); Gerhard O. Forde, *On Being a Theologian of the Cross: Reflections on Luther's Heidelberg Disputation, 1518* (Grand Rapids, MI: Eerdmans, 1997); Solberg, *Compelling Knowledge*; Douglas John Hall, *The Cross in Our Context: Jesus and the Suffering World* (Minneapolis: Augsburg Fortress, 2003); Mark W. Thomsen, *Christ Crucified: A 21st-Century Missiology of the Cross* (Minneapolis: Lutheran University Press, 2004); Deanna A. Thompson, *Crossing the Divide: Luther, Feminism, and the Cross* (Minneapolis: Augsburg Fortress, 2004); John D. Caputo, *The Weakness of God: A Theology of the Event* (Bloomington: Indiana University Press, 2006); Vítor Westhelle, *The Scandalous God: The Use and Abuse of the Cross* (Minneapolis: Fortress, 2006); Anna Madsen, *The Theology of the Cross in Historical Perspective* (Eugene, OR: Wipf & Stock, 2007); David A. Brondos, *Fortress Introduction to Salvation and the Cross* (Minneapolis: Fortress, 2007); Phil Ruge-Jones, *The Word of the Cross in a World of Glory* (Minneapolis: Augsburg Fortress, 2008); Philip Ruge-Jones, *Cross in Tensions: Luther's Theology of the Cross as Theological-Social Critique* (Eugene, OR: Pickwick, 2008); Theodore W. Jennings Jr., *Transforming Atonement: A Political Theology of the Cross* (Minneapolis: Fortress, 2009); Neal J. Anthony, *Cross Narratives: Martin Luther's Christology and the Location of Redemption* (Eugene, OR: Wipf & Stock, 2010); Andrew Root, *The Promise of Despair: The Way of the Cross as the Way of the Church* (Nashville, TN: Abingdon, 2010); Robert Cady Saler, *Theologia Crucis: A Companion to the Theology of the Cross* (Eugene, OR: Cascade, 2016); Dennis Ngien, *Luther's Theology of the Cross: Christ in Luther's Sermons on John* (Eugene, OR: Cascade, 2018); and John D. Caputo, *The Cross and Cosmos: A Theology of Difficult Glory* (Bloomington: Indiana University Press, 2019).

18 Moltmann, *Crucified God*, 4.

19 See Hall, *Lighten Our Darkness*, 43–59.

20 Hall, 149.

21 For a discussion of several of these works, see Craig L. Nessan, "Thine Is the Kingdom, the Power, and the Glory: New Vistas for the Theology of the Cross," *Dialog* 50 (Spring 2011): 81–89.

22 Enrique Dussel, A *History of the Church in Latin America: Colonialism to Liberation (1492–1979)*, trans. Alan Neely (Grand Rapids, MI: Eerdmans, 1981), 307.

23 Solberg, *Compelling Knowledge*, 125.

24 "Citizens United Explained," Brennan Center for Justice, accessed September 22, 2020, https://www.brennancenter.org/our-work/research-reports/citizens-united-explained.

25 Cf. Nessan, *Shalom Church*.

26 Bonhoeffer, "View from Below," 17.

27 Dietrich Bonhoeffer, "The Church and the Jewish Question," in *Dietrich Bonhoeffer Works: Berlin 1932–1933*, ed. Larry L. Rasmussen, trans. Isabel Best and David Higgins (Minneapolis: Fortress, 2009), 12:365–66.

Chapter Eight

1 See Johannes Heckel, *Lex Charitatis: A Juristic Disquisition on Law in the Theology of Martin Luther*, trans. Gerhard G. Krodel (Grand Rapids, MI: Eerdmans, 2010).

2 Cf. Hertz, *Two Kingdoms*.

3 For example, see the explanation of social teaching by the Evangelical Lutheran Church in America, "The Church in Society: A Lutheran Perspective," Evangelical Lutheran Church in America, accessed February 18, 2017, http://download.elca.org/ELCA%20Resource%20Repository/Church_SocietySS.pdf?_ga=1.146091956.1660177343.1378417152.

4 For a compelling portrait of Luther's worldview, see Oberman, *Luther*.

5 Cf. Walter Wink, *The Powers That Be: Theology for a New Millennium* (New York: Doubleday, 1999).

6 Bliese and Gelder, *Evangelizing Church*, chap. 7.

7 Nessan, "Neighborliness (*Diakonia*)," 143–46.

8 Cf. Paul Tillich, *Love, Power, and Justice* (New York: Oxford University Press, 1954), 71.

9 Nessan, *Shalom Church*, chap. 3.

10 Lohse, *Martin Luther's Theology*, 184, 270.

11 Lohse, 271.

12 Althaus, *Theology of Martin Luther*, 253–55; Oswald Bayer, *Martin Luther's Theology: A Contemporary Interpretation*, trans. Thomas H. Trapp (Grand Rapids, MI: Eerdmans, 2008), 61n27.

13 Althaus, *Theology of Martin Luther*, 227.

14 Paul Althaus, *The Ethics of Martin Luther*, trans. Robert C. Schultz (Philadelphia: Fortress, 1972), 49–50. The citations within the quote are from LW 46:99–100 and LW 21:26.

15 LW 51:374.

16 LW 33:290.

17 LW 34:137.

18 See the several essays underscoring the value of reason in the Lutheran tradition in Jennifer Hockenbery Dragseth, ed., *The Devil's Whore: Reason and Philosophy in the Lutheran Tradition* (Minneapolis: Fortress, 2011).

19 Cf. Richard W. Solberg, *Lutheran Higher Education in North America* (Minneapolis: Augsburg, 1985).

20 LW 32:112.

21 LW 33:288–89. For further commentary, see Bayer, *Martin Luther's Theology*, 185–92.

22 LW 33:70.

23 LW 31:25–33. Other forms of pious works earning merit included worshipping saints, pilgrimages to shrines, private masses without communicants, and venerating relics.

24 For this and the previous citation, LW 31:346–47.

25 LW 31:344.

26 Cf. LW 44:23–39.

27 LW 31:344.

28 LW 33:364–65.

29 LW 44:80–114.

30 Mead, *Lively Experiment*.

31 Other church bodies in particular contexts also may operate in this fashion—for example, when the Roman Catholic Church engages in advocacy according to the logic of Christendom.

Conclusion

1 "Confession and Forgiveness," 95.

2 Paul Tillich, *Systematic Theology*, vol. 1, *Reason and Revelation, Being and God* (Chicago: University of Chicago Press, 1951), 114.

3 See Arden F. Mahlberg and Craig L. Nessan, *The Integrity of the Body of Christ: Boundary Keeping as Shared Responsibility* (Eugene, OR: Wipf & Stock, 2016), 85–94.

4 "25 CBT Techniques and Worksheets for Cognitive Behavioral Therapy," Positive Psychology, accessed October 12, 2020, https://positivepsychology.com/

cbt-cognitive-behavioral-therapy-techniques-worksheets/#:~:text=Cognitive
%20Distortions%201%20Filtering.%20Filtering%20refers%20to%20the,of
%20gray.%203%20Overgeneralization.%20...%20More%20items...%20.

5   Cf. Martin Luther, "How Christians Should Regard Moses," in Stjerna, *Annotated Luther*, 2:143.

6   "Universal Declaration of Human Rights," United Nations, accessed October 8, 2020, https://www.un.org/en/about-us/universal-declaration-of-human-rights.

7   On the lasting physical effects of trauma, see Bessel A. van der Kolk, *The Body Keeps the Score: Brain, Mind, and Body in the Healing of Trauma* (New York: Penguin, 2014).

8   For example, William A. Darity and A. Kirsten Mullen, *From Here to Equality: Reparations for Black Americans in the Twenty-First Century* (Chapel Hill: University of North Carolina Press, 2020).

9   Reinhold Niebuhr, *The Irony of American History* (New York: Charles Scribner's Sons, 1952), 63.

10 Cf. J. Richard Middleton, *The Liberating Image: The* Imago Dei *in Genesis 1* (Grand Rapids, MI: Brazos, 2005), 64–66, 126–28, 182–83.

Selected Bibliography

Ethics and Scripture

Birch, Bruce C., Jacqueline E. Lapsley, Cynthia Moe-Lobeda, and Larry L. Rasmussen. *Bible and Ethics in the Christian Life: A New Conversation*. Minneapolis: Fortress, 2018.

Fedler, Kyle D. *Exploring Christian Ethics: Biblical Foundations for Morality*. Louisville, KY: John Knox, 2006.

Janzen, Waldemar. *Old Testament Ethics: A Paradigmatic Approach*. Louisville, KY: Westminster John Knox, 1994.

Jersild, Paul. *Spirit Ethics: Scripture and the Moral Life*. Minneapolis: Fortress, 2000.

Jones, David W. *An Introduction to Biblical Ethics*. Nashville, TN: B&H Academic, 2013.

Kelsey, David H. *The Uses of Scripture in Recent Theology*. Philadelphia: Fortress, 1975.

Sider, Ronald J. *Cry Justice: The Bible on Hunger and Poverty*. New York: Paulist, 1980.

Siker, Jeffrey S. *Scripture and Ethics: Twentieth-Century Portraits*. New York: Oxford University Press, 1997.

Spohn, William C. *What Are They Saying about Scripture and Ethics?* New York: Paulist, 1995.

Ethics of the New Testament

Furnish, Victor Paul. *Theology and Ethics in Paul*. Nashville, TN: Abingdon, 1986.

Harvey, A. E. *Strenuous Commands: The Ethic of Jesus*. Philadelphia: Trinity, 1990.

Hays, Richard B. *The Moral Vision of the New Testament*. San Francisco: HarperCollins, 1996.

Kaminouchi, Alberto de Mingo. *An Introduction to Christian Ethics: A New Testament Perspective.* Collegeville, MN: Liturgical, 2020.

Lohse, Eduard. *Theological Ethics of the New Testament.* Translated by M. Eugene Boring. Minneapolis: Fortress, 1991.

Marxsen, Willi. *New Testament Foundations for Christian Ethics.* Translated by O. C. Dean Jr. Minneapolis: Fortress, 1993.

Matera, Frank J. *New Testament Ethics: The Legacies of Jesus and Paul.* Louisville, KY: Westminster John Knox, 1996.

Schrage, Wolfgang. *The Ethics of the New Testament.* Translated by David E. Green. Philadelphia: Fortress, 1988.

Theissen, Gerd. *Social Reality and the Early Christians: Theology, Ethics, and the World of the New Testament.* Translated by Margaret Kohl. Minneapolis: Fortress, 1992.

Witherington, Ben. *New Testament Theology and Ethics.* Downers Grove, IL: InterVarsity, 2016.

Historical Perspectives

Forell, George W. *Christian Social Teachings: A Reader in Christian Social Ethics from the Bible to the Present.* Minneapolis: Augsburg, 1971.

———. *History of Christian Ethics.* Vol. 1, *From the New Testament to Augustine.* Minneapolis: Augsburg, 1979.

Gill, Robin. *A Textbook of Christian Ethics.* Edinburgh: T&T Clark, 1995.

MacIntyre, Alasdair. *A Short History of Ethics: A History of Moral Philosophy from the Homeric Age to the Twentieth Century.* New York: Simon & Schuster, 1966.

Meeks, Wayne A. *The Origins of Christian Morality: The First Two Centuries.* New Haven, CT: Yale University Press, 1993.

Wogaman, J. Philip. *Christian Ethics: A Historical Introduction.* Louisville, KY: Westminster John Knox, 1993.

Wogaman, J. Philip, and Douglas M. Strong. *Readings in Christian Ethics: A Historical Sourcebook.* Louisville, KY: Westminster John Knox, 1996.

Ethics in the Lutheran Tradition

Althaus, Paul. *The Ethics of Martin Luther.* Translated by Robert C. Schultz. Philadelphia: Fortress, 1972.

Altmann, Walter. *Luther and Liberation: A Latin American Perspective.* 2nd ed. Minneapolis: Fortress, 2015.

Bayer, Oswald. *Freedom in Response: Lutheran Ethics: Sources and Controversies.* Translated by Jeffrey Cayzer. New York: Oxford University Press, 2007.

Biermann, Joel D. *A Case for Character: Towards a Lutheran Virtue Ethics.* Minneapolis: Fortress, 2014.

Bloomquist, Karen L., ed. *Lutheran Ethics at the Intersections of God's One World.* Geneva: Lutheran World Federation, 2005.

Bloomquist, Karen L., and John R. Stumme, eds. *The Promise of Lutheran Ethics.* Minneapolis: Fortress, 1998.

Bonhoeffer, Dietrich. *Ethics.* Edited by Clifford J. Green. Translated by Reinhard Krauss, Charles C. West, and Douglas W. Stott. Dietrich Bonhoeffer Works 6. Minneapolis: Fortress, 2005.

Elert, Werner. *The Christian Ethos: The Foundations of the Christian Way of Life.* Translated by Carl J. Schindler. Philadelphia: Muhlenberg, 1957.

Forell, George Wolfgang. *Faith Active in Love: An Investigation of the Principles Underlying Luther's Social Ethics.* New York: American Press, 1954.

Larson, Steven, H. Paul Santmire, and Samuel Torvend. *What Are the Ethical Implications of Worship?* Minneapolis: Augsburg Fortress, 1996.

Lazareth, William H. *Christians in Society: Luther, the Bible, and Social Ethics.* Minneapolis: Fortress, 2001.

Letts, Harold C. *Existence Today: Christian Social Responsibility.* Vol. 1. Philadelphia: Muhlenberg, 1957.

———. *Life in Community: Christian Social Responsibility.* Vol. 3. Philadelphia: Muhlenberg, 1957.

———. *The Lutheran Heritage: Christian Social Responsibility.* Vol. 2. Philadelphia: Muhlenberg, 1957.

Moe-Lobeda, Cynthia D. *Public Church: For the Life of the World.* Minneapolis: Augsburg Fortress, 2004.

Solberg, Mary M. *Compelling Knowledge: A Feminist Proposal for an Epistemology of the Cross.* New York: State University of New York Press, 1997.

Stumme, John R., and Robert W. Tuttle, eds. *Church and State: Lutheran Perspectives.* Minneapolis: Fortress, 2003.

Vajta, Vilmos, ed. *The Gospel and Human Destiny.* Minneapolis: Augsburg, 1971.

Wengert, Timothy J. *Harvesting Martin Luther's Reflections on Theology, Ethics, and the Church.* Grand Rapids, MI: Eerdmans, 2004.

Theological Ethics

Baker-Fletcher, Garth Kasimu. *Dirty Hands: Christian Ethics in a Morally Ambiguous World.* Minneapolis: Fortress, 2000.

Bloesch, Donald G. *Freedom for Obedience: Evangelical Ethics for Contemporary Times.* San Francisco: Harper & Row, 1987.

Bloomquist, Karen L., Craig L. Nessan, and Hans Ulrich, eds. *Radicalizing Reformation: North American Perspectives.* Zürich: Lit Verlag, 2016.

Burtness, James H. *Consequences: Morality, Ethics, and the Future.* Minneapolis: Fortress, 1999.

Cahill, Lisa Sowle, and James F. Childress. *Christian Ethics: Problems and Prospects.* Cleveland: Pilgrim Press, 1996.

Childs, James M., Jr. *Ethics in the Community of Promise: Faith, Formation, and Decision.* Rev. ed. Minneapolis: Fortress, 2006.

Fletcher, Joseph. *Situation Ethics: The New Morality.* Louisville, KY: Westminster John Knox, 1997.

Gill, Robin, ed. *The Cambridge Companion to Christian Ethics.* Cambridge: Cambridge University Press, 2001.

Grudem, Wayne. *Christian Ethics: An Introduction to Biblical Moral Reasoning.* Wheaton, IL: Crossway, 2018.

Gustafson, James M. *Ethics from a Theocentric Perspective.* Vol. 1, *Theology and Ethics.* Chicago: University of Chicago Press, 1981.

———. *Ethics from a Theocentric Perspective.* Vol. 2, *Ethics and Theology.* Chicago: University of Chicago Press, 1981.

———. *Moral Discernment in the Christian Life: Essays in Theological Ethics.* Louisville, KY: Westminster John Knox, 2007.

Häring, Bernard. *Free and Faithful in Christ.* Vol. 1, *General Moral Theology.* New York: Seabury, 1978.

———. *Free and Faithful in Christ.* Vol. 2, *The Truth Will Set You Free.* New York: Crossroad, 1979.

———. *Free and Faithful in Christ.* Vol. 3, *Light to the World.* New York: Crossroad, 1981.

Hastings, W. Ross. *Theological Ethics: The Moral Life of the Gospel in Contemporary Context.* Grand Rapids, MI: Zondervan Academic, 2021.

Hauerwas, Stanley. *The Hauerwas Reader.* Edited by John Berkman and Michael Cartwright. Durham, NC: Duke University Press, 2001.

———. *The Peaceable Kingdom.* Notre Dame, IN: University of Notre Dame Press, 1983.

Hauerwas, Stanley, and Samuel Wells, eds. *The Blackwell Companion to Christian Ethics.* Oxford: Blackwell, 2004.

Jackelén, Antje. *God Is Greater: Theology for the World.* Minneapolis: Fortress, 2020.

Jersild, Paul. *Making Moral Decisions: A Christian Approach to Personal and Social Ethics.* Minneapolis: Fortress, 1990.

Lehmann, Paul. *Ethics in a Christian Context.* New York: Harper & Row, 1963.

Løgstrup, Knud Ejler. *The Ethical Demand.* Translated by T. I. Jensen, Gary Puckering, and Eric Watkins. Notre Dame, IN: University of Notre Dame Press, 1997.

Long, D. Stephen. *Christian Ethics: A Very Short Introduction.* New York: Oxford University Press, 2010.

Lovin, Robin W. *An Introduction to Christian Ethics: Goals, Duties, and Virtues.* Nashville, TN: Abingdon, 2011.

MacIntyre, Alasdair. *After Virtue: A Study in Moral Theory.* Notre Dame, IN: University of Notre Dame Press, 2007.

———. *Whose Justice? Which Rationality?* Notre Dame, IN: University of Notre Dame Press, 1988.

Maguire, Daniel C. *The Moral Core of Judaism and Christianity: Reclaiming the Revolution.* Minneapolis: Fortress, 1993.

McClendon, James Wm., Jr. *Systematic Theology: Ethics.* Nashville, TN: Abingdon, 1986.

Meilaender, Gilbert C. *Faith and Faithfulness: Basic Themes in Christian Ethics.* Notre Dame, IN: University of Notre Dame Press, 1991.

Meilaender, Gilbert, and William Werpehowsik, eds. *The Oxford Handbook of Theological Ethics.* Oxford: Oxford University Press, 2005.

Mescher, Marcus. *The Ethics of Encounter: Christian Neighbor Love as a Practice of Solidarity.* Maryknoll, NY: Orbis, 2020.

Moltmann, Jürgen. *On Human Dignity: Political Ethics and Theology.* Translated by M. Douglas Meeks. Minneapolis: Fortress, 2007.

Nelson, James B. *Moral Nexus: Ethics of Christian Identity and Community.* Louisville, KY: Westminster John Knox, 1996.

Nessan, Craig L. *Shalom Church: The Body of Christ as Ministering Community.* Minneapolis: Fortress, 2010.

Niebuhr, Reinhold. *An Interpretation of Christian Ethics.* New York: Meridian, 1956.

Pannenberg, Wolfhart. *Ethics.* Translated by Keith Crim. Philadelphia: Westminster, 1981.

Paris, Peter J. *African American Theological Ethics.* Louisville, KY: Westminster John Knox, 2016.

Pieper, Josef. *The Four Cardinal Virtues.* Translated by Daniel F. Coogan, Lawrence E. Lynch, Clara Winston, and Richard Winston. Notre Dame, IN: University of Notre Dame Press, 1966.

Rendtorff, Trutz. *Ethics.* Vol. 1, *Basic Elements and Methodology in an Ethical Theology.* Translated by Keith Crim. Philadelphia: Fortress, 1986.

———. *Ethics.* Vol. 2, *Applications of an Ethical Theology.* Translated by Keith Crim. Philadelphia: Fortress, 1989.

Salzman, Todd A., and Michael G. Lawler. *Virtue and Theological Ethics: Toward a Renewed Ethical Method.* Maryknoll, NY: Orbis, 2018.

Sittler, Joseph. *The Structure of Christian Ethics.* Baton Rouge: Louisiana State University Press, 1958.

Stone, Ronald H. *The Ultimate Imperative: An Interpretation of Christian Ethics.* Cleveland: Pilgrim Press, 1999.

Thielicke, Helmut. *Theological Ethics.* Vol. 1, *Foundations.* Edited and translated by William H. Lazareth. Philadelphia: Fortress, 1966.

———. *Theological Ethics*. Vol. 2, *Politics*. Edited and translated by William H. Lazareth. Philadelphia: Fortress, 1969.

Webster, John. *Barth's Moral Theology: Human Action in Barth's Thought*. Grand Rapids, MI: Eerdmans, 1998.

Wells, Samuel Wells, Ben Quash, and Rebekah Eklund. *Introducing Christian Ethics*. 2nd ed. Oxford: Wiley Blackwell, 2017.

Wogaman, J. Philip. *Christian Moral Judgment*. Louisville, KY: Westminster John Knox, 1989.

Social Ethics

Bieler, Andrea, and Hans-Martin Gutmann. *Embodying Grace: Proclaiming Justification in the Real World*. Translated by L. Maloney. Minneapolis: Fortress, 2010.

Braaten, Carl E., and Robert W. Jenson, eds. *The Two Cities of God: The Church's Responsibility for the Earthly City*. Grand Rapids, MI: Eerdmans, 1997.

Cannon, Katie Geneva, Emilie M. Townes, and Angela D. Sims, eds. *Womanist Theological Ethics: A Reader*. Louisville, KY: Westminster John Knox, 2011.

Christie, Dolores L. *Moral Choice: A Christian View of Ethics*. Minneapolis: Fortress, 2013.

De La Torre, Miguel A. *Doing Christian Ethics from the Margins*. 2nd ed. Maryknoll, NY: Orbis, 2014.

DeYoung, Curtiss Paul. *Living Faith: How Faith Inspires Social Justice*. Minneapolis: Fortress, 2007.

Hoehn, Richard A. *Up from Apathy: A Study of Moral Awareness and Social Involvement*. Nashville, TN: Abingdon, 1983.

Holland, Joe, and Peter Henriot. *Social Analysis: Linking Faith and Justice*. Washington, DC: Center of Concerns, 1986.

Lloyd, Vincent W., and Andrew Prevot, eds. *Anti-Blackness and Christian Ethics*. Maryknoll, NY: Orbis, 2017.

Maguire, Daniel C. *Ethics: A Complete Method for Moral Choice*. Minneapolis: Fortress, 2010.

———. *A Moral Creed for All Christians*. Minneapolis: Fortress, 2005.

Nessan, Craig L. *The Vitality of Liberation Theology*. Eugene, OR: Wipf & Stock, 2012.

Ogletree, Thomas W. *The World Calling: The Church's Witness in Politics and Society*. Louisville, KY: Westminster John Knox, 2004.

Quanbeck, Warren A. *God and Caesar: A Christian Approach to Social Ethics*. Minneapolis: Augsburg, 1959.

Schubeck, Thomas L., S. J. *Liberation Ethics: Sources, Models, and Norms*. Minneapolis: Fortress, 1993.

Stassen, Glen H., and David P. Gushee. *Kingdom Ethics: Following Jesus in Contemporary Context*. Downers Grove, IL: InterVarsity, 2003.

Williams, Reggie L. *Bonhoeffer's Black Jesus: Harlem Renaissance Theology and an Ethic of Resistance*. Waco, TX: Baylor University Press, 2014.

Wogaman, J. Philip. *Christian Perspectives on Politics*. Louisville, KY: Westminster John Knox, 2000.

Special Topics

Barbour, Ian. *Ethics in an Age of Technology, the Gifford Lectures 1989–1991*. Vol. 2. San Francisco: HarperCollins, 1964.

Cahill, Lisa Sowle. *Blessed Are the Peacemakers: Pacifism, Just War, and Peacebuilding*. Minneapolis: Fortress, 2019.

———. *Sex, Gender, and Christian Ethics*. New York: Cambridge University Press, 1996.

Cannon, Katie G. *Black Womanist Ethics*. Atlanta: Scholars, 1988.

Childs, James M., Jr. *Aging and Loving: Christian Faith and Sexuality in Later Life*. Minneapolis: Fortress, 2021.

———. *Ethics in Business: Faith at Work*. Minneapolis: Fortress, 1995.

———. *Greed: Economics and Ethics in Conflict*. Minneapolis: Fortress, 2000.

———. *The Way of Peace: Christian Life in Face of Discord*. Minneapolis: Fortress, 2008.

Clapham, Andrew. *Human Rights: A Very Short Introduction*. Oxford: Oxford University Press, 2007.

Clayton, Philip, and Jeffrey Schloss, eds. *Evolution and Ethics: Human Morality in Biological and Religious Perspective*. Grand Rapids, MI: Eerdmans, 2004.

Daly, Lois K., ed. *Feminist Theological Ethics: A Reader*. Louisville, KY: Westminster John Knox, 1994.

Duchrow, Ulrich. *Alternatives to Global Capitalism: Drawn from Biblical History Designed for Political Action*. Translated by Elizabeth Hicks. Geneva: WCC, 1987.

———. *Global Economy: A Confessional Issue for the Churches?* Translated by David Lewis. Geneva: WCC, 1987.

Edwards, Andres R. *The Sustainability Revolution: Portrait of a Paradigm Shift*. Gabriola Island, BC: New Society, 2005.

Grenz, Stanley J. *Sexual Ethics: An Evangelical Perspective*. Louisville, KY: Westminster John Knox, 1990.

Gudorf, Christine E. *Body, Sex, and Pleasure: Reconstructing Christian Sexual Ethics*. Cleveland: Pilgrim Press, 1994.

Gula, Richard M. *Ethics in Pastoral Ministry*. New York: Paulist, 1996.

Hamburger, Philip. *Separation of Church and State*. Cambridge, MA: Harvard University Press, 2002.

Henderson-Espinosa, Robyn. *Activist Theology*. Minneapolis: Fortress, 2019.

Jackson, Timothy P. *The Morality of Adoption: Social-Psychological, Theological, and Legal Perspectives*. Grand Rapids, MI: Eerdmans, 2005.

Jenkins, Willis. *Ecologies of Grace: Environmental Ethics and Christian Theology*. New York: Oxford University Press, 2008.

———. *The Future of Ethics: Sustainability, Social Justice, and Religious Creativity*. Washington, DC: Georgetown University Press, 2013.

Johnson, Mark. *Moral Imagination: Implications of Cognitive Science for Ethics*. Chicago: University of Chicago Press, 1993.

Lammers, Stephen E., and Allen Verhey, eds. *Moral Medicine: Theological Perspectives in Medical Ethics*. 2nd ed. Grand Rapids, MI: Eerdmans, 1998.

Maguire, Daniel C. *The Horrors We Bless: Rethinking the Just-War Legacy*. Minneapolis: Fortress, 2007.

Mahlberg, Arden, and Craig L. Nessan. *The Integrity of the Body of Christ: Boundary Keeping as Shared Responsibility*. Eugene, OR: Wipf & Stock, 2016.

McFague, Sallie. *A New Climate for Theology: God, the World, and Global Warming*. Minneapolis: Fortress, 2008.

Meilaender, Gilbert. *Bioethics: A Primer for Christians*. Grand Rapids, MI: Eerdmans, 2005.

Nkansah-Obrempong, James. *Foundations for African Theological Ethics*. Carlisle, UK: Langham, 2013.

Owens, Erik C., John D. Carlson, and Eric P. Elshtain, eds. *Religion and the Death Penalty: A Call for Reckoning*. Grand Rapids, MI: Eerdmans, 2004.

Peppard, Christiana Z. *Just Water: Theology, Ethics, and the Global Water Crisis*. Maryknoll, NY: Orbis, 2014.

Peters, Ted. *For the Love of Children: Genetic Technology and the Future of the Family*. Louisville, KY: Westminster John Knox, 1996.

———. *Playing God? Genetic Determinism and Human Freedom*. New York: Routledge, 1997.

Rawls, John. *A Theory of Justice*. 2nd ed. Cambridge, MA: Belknap, 1999.

Roth, John K., ed. *Ethics after the Holocaust: Perspectives, Critiques, and Responses*. St. Paul, MN: Paragon, 1999.

Santmire, H. Paul. *Ritualizing Nature: Renewing Christian Liturgy in a Time of Crisis*. Minneapolis: Fortress, 2008.

Schafer-Landau, Russ, ed. *Ethical Theory: An Anthology*. Oxford: Blackwell, 2007.

Schweiker, William, and Charles Mathewes, eds. *Having: Property and Possession in Religious and Social Life*. Grand Rapids, MI: Eerdmans, 2004.

Shannon, Thomas A., ed. *Death and Dying: A Reader*. Lanham, MD: Sheed & Ward, 2004.

———, ed. *Reproductive Technologies: A Reader*. Lanham, MD: Sheed & Ward, 2004.

Sider, Ronald J. *Christ and Violence*. Scottdale, PA: Herald, 1997.

———. *Rich Christians in an Age of Hunger: A Biblical Study*. Downers Grove, IL: Inter-Varsity, 1979.

Simpson, Gary M. *War, Peace, and God: Rethinking the Just-War Tradition*. Minneapolis: Augsburg Fortress, 2007.

Stivers, Laura A., and James B. Martin-Schramm, eds. *Christian Ethics: A Case Method Approach*. 5th ed. Maryknoll, NY: Orbis, 2020.

Sullivan, William M., and Will Kymlicka, eds. *The Globalization of Ethics: Religious and Secular Perspectives*. New York: Cambridge University Press, 2007.

Thielicke, Helmut. *The Ethics of Sex*. Translated by John W. Doberstein. Grand Rapids, MI: Baker, 1964.

Thurow, Roger. *Enough: Why the World's Poorest Starve in an Age of Plenty*. Philadelphia: Public Affairs, 2010.

Unruh, Heidi Rolland, and Ronald J. Sider. *Saving Souls, Serving Society: Understanding the Faith Factor in Church-Based Social Ministry*. New York: Oxford University Press, 2005.

Welch, Sharon D. *A Feminist Ethic of Risk*. Minneapolis: Fortress, 1990.

———. *Real Peace, Real Security: The Challenges of Global Citizenship*. Minneapolis: Fortress, 2008.

West, Tracie C. *Disruptive Christian Ethics: When Racism and Women's Lives Matter*. Louisville, KY: Westminster John Knox, 2006.

Woodley, Randy. *Shalom and the Community of Creation: An Indigenous Vision*. Grand Rapids, MI: Eerdmans, 2012.

Interreligious Themes

Carmody, Denis Lardner, and John Tully Carmody. *Peace and Justice in the Scriptures of the World Religions*. Mahwah, NJ: Paulist, 1988.

Hunsinger, George, ed. *Torture Is a Moral Issue: Christians, Jews, Muslims, and People of Conscience Speak Out*. Grand Rapids, MI: Eerdmans, 2008.

Küng, Hans, ed. *Yes to a Global Ethic*. New York: Continuum, 1996.

Küng, Hans, and Karl-Josef Kuschel, eds. *A Global Ethic: The Declaration of the Parliament of the World's Religions*. New York: Continuum, 1993.

LaHurd, Carol Schersten, ed. *Engaging Others, Knowing Ourselves: A Lutheran Calling in a Multi-religious World*. Minneapolis: Lutheran University Press, 2016.

Maguire, Daniel C. *Sacred Energies: When the World's Religions Sit Down to Talk about the Future of Human Life and the Plight of This Planet*. Minneapolis: Fortress, 2000.

Volf, Miroslav, Ghazi bin Muhammad, and Melissa Yarrington, eds. *A Common Word: Muslims and Christians on Loving God and Neighbor*. Grand Rapids, MI: Eerdmans, 2010.

Subject Index